Being Liberal in an Illiberal Age

Being Liberal in an Illiberal Age

Why I am a Unitarian Universalist

Second Edition

Jack Mendelsohn

SKINNER HOUSE BOOKS

BOSTON

Published by Skinner House Books. Skinner House Books is an imprint of the
Unitarian Universalist Association of Congregations, a liberal religious organiza-
tion with more than 1,000 congregations in the U.S. and Canada. 25 Beacon
Street, Boston, MA 02108-2800.

Printed in United States.

ISBN 1-55896-505-X
978-1-55896-505-8

This book was originally published in 1964 by Beacon Press and updated as late
as 1985. It became a Skinner House Books publication in 1995.

We gratefully acknowledge permission to reprint the following:

"The Star Splitter," by Robert Frost, copyright 1923, 1969 by Henry Holt and
Company, copyright 1951 by Robert Frost. *The Poetry of Robert Frost* edited by
Edward Connery Lathem. Reprinted by permission of Henry Holt and
Company, LLC.

Excerpt from "The Man with the Blue Guitar," in *The Collected Poems of Wallace
Stevens* by Wallace Stevens, copyright 1954 by Wallace Stevens and renewed
1982 by Holly Stevens. Used by permission of Alfred A. Knopf, a division of
Random House, Inc.

Excerpt from "Man, the Moon Shooter" in *The Complete Poems of Carl
Sandburg*, copyright © 1970, 1969 by Lilian Steichen Sandburg, Trustee,
reprinted by permission of Harcourt, Inc.

Excerpt from *J.B.: A Play in Verse* by Archibald MacLeish. Copyright © 1958 by
Archibald MacLeish, renewed 1986 by William H. MacLeish and Mary H. Grimm.
Reprinted by permission of Houghton Mifflin Company. All rights reserved.

08 07 06
5 4 3 2 1

Library of Congress Cataloging-in-Publication Data
Mendelsohn, Jack, 1918-
    Being liberal in an illiberal age : why I am a Unitarian Universalist / Jack
Mendelsohn.—2nd ed.
        p. cm.
    Includes index.
    ISBN-13: 978-1-55896-505-8 (pbk. : alk. paper)
    ISBN-10: 1-55896-505-X (pbk. : alk. paper)
    1. Unitarian Universalist Association—Apologetic works. 2. Liberalism
(Religion)—Unitarian Universalist churches. 3. Mendelsohn, Jack, 1918- I.
Title.

BX9841.2.M46 2006
289.1'32—dc22

2005036222

To all those, living and dead,
who are my beloved liberal companions.
Like the wild asses in the 39th chapter of Job,
we roam the barren wilderness
searching after every green thing.

Contents

Foreword

I'll always be grateful to Jack Mendelsohn for introducing me to Unitarian Universalism. It was the late sixties, and I was a college student at Yale. Our chaplain was the Reverend William Sloane Coffin, Jr., a nationally known civil rights and peace activist. Coffin had attended a huge anti-war gathering at the Unitarian Universalist church Jack was then serving in Boston. "Long on ethics," Coffin had said of Unitarian Universalism and its flagship Arlington Street Church.

At the time, I'd been struggling for a couple of years over my faith (I was then a Presbyterian), or lack of it, in seminars and pastoral counseling sessions with Coffin, who was also a Presbyterian. "How can a just and caring deity allow 'acts of God' like earthquakes, tidal waves, and hurricanes to kill innocent people?" I'd ask. "How can a loving and compassionate God condemn anyone eternally to hell?" I wanted to know why people couldn't be saved just as well through religions other than Christianity. My biggest problem, though, was how Jesus could have been fully divine—rather than just a great human teacher and prophet, like Moses or Buddha or Muhammad. After a number of exasperating sessions (I'm sure as much for Coffin as for me) he finally exclaimed, "Go check out the Unitarian Universalists! They seem to think like you and talk like you. Maybe they'll have a home for you."

With Jack's book in my hands, I was soon mesmerized. This is a religion? A free faith without any dogma or doctrine binding its followers? God can be understood not as an authority figure but as the laws of nature? The highest form of love is so unconditional that it ultimately condemns no one to hell? Unitarian Universalists respect all of the major religious traditions of the world, as well as non-religious traditions like humanism and rationalism? Jesus was indeed a great human teacher and prophet but not God? What really matters is how you live this life, not speculation about an afterlife?

Bill Coffin's complete comment about Unitarian Universalism had been, "Long on ethics, but short on theology." But that was just fine with me. I'd been yearning for a religion that was primarily concerned with how to live a good and fulfilling life, here and now. I was much less interested in esoteric theology about a judgmental God who sends people to heaven or to hell or miraculously intervenes in the natural order. Through Unitarian Universalism, I came to understand that not all Christians see their own faith this way either. But through Jack Mendelsohn's book, I truly began to understand the nature of liberal religion, whatever the label.

In the years that followed I came to know Jack quite well as a colleague and friend. By then I had graduated from law school and divinity school, become a lawyer and Unitarian Universalist minister myself, and was providing church-sponsored legal services in a low-income neighborhood in Boston. Jack was very supportive of my work—through the church he was then serving in a Boston suburb and through his leadership in our local district as well as our continental denomination. By then I'd come to appreciate his true status, not only in our religious movement but nationally and internationally in causes like racial justice, mediation in international conflict (especially in the Middle East), economic justice, feminism, and the rights of gay, lesbian, bisexual and transgender people. At the same time, Jack was an outstanding preacher, pastor, scholar, and teacher—all of one piece, woven fine on the loom of his spiritual conviction. Jack was a tremendous institutional figure in Unitarian Universalism: He had been a candidate for the presidency of the Unitarian Universalist Association, president of the UU Ministers Association, and vice president of the UU Service Committee, and he had chaired countless committees and task forces. Personally, he was warm and caring. As a public figure, he was as strong and effective an advocate for social justice as you'd ever want at your side. At the same time, his sense of good humor was always reliable and his laugh broad and infectious.

Jack Mendelsohn first became a minister more than sixty years ago. *Being Liberal in an Illiberal Age* was first published in 1960 under the title *Why I Am a Unitarian*, and it has been revised a few times since. The book is a classic, but it is now more than ever on the cutting edge. These are certainly illiberal times, and Jack's un-apologetic celebration of liberalism is greatly needed in this first decade of the new millennium. The very word liberal needs to be reclaimed and affirmed in its positive sense. Conservatives frame the word to connote licentiousness and chaos. Radicals on the left construct it to mean tolerant complacency and hypocrisy. Jack Mendelsohn calls us to see liberalism as an active hunger for freedom, equality, and justice—spiritual values that have always been at the center of Unitarian Universalism—coupled with a disciplined organizing capability to see those values effectively institutionalized in society.

This book is a primer on liberal religion, full of examples and stories, history and vision. I remember how exciting it was for me to learn about some of the exemplars of Unitarian Universalism since the American Revolution: five U.S. presidents, starting with John Adams and Thomas Jefferson; literary figures like the Longfellows, Ralph Waldo Emerson, Louisa May Alcott, and Margaret Fuller; women's rights advocates like Elizabeth Cady Stanton and Susan B. Anthony; humanitarians like Clara Barton, Julia Ward Howe, and Whitney Young. Reading Jack's book, I learned about a church that has always respected reason and the scientific method, a church that affirms truth as always incomplete and emerging rather than revealed and complete, a church that appreciates the role of doubt and questioning, a church that puts fellowship with others who are different ahead of conformity with those who share the same beliefs.

At this time in history, liberalism as exemplified in Unitarian Universalism has a critical social role to play. Various fundamentalisms and orthodoxies are holding sway, and worldwide misunderstanding and outright warfare between religions are on the rise. Unitarian Universalists have a history of understanding the great world religions and their interrelationships. UUs demonstrate dynamic appreciation of different traditions within our own congregations while modeling pluralism, inclusivity, and a commitment to living out our faith in the world. At our best, we should be able to provide both the vision and the methods to promote the kind of deep, empathetic dialogue and understanding that leads to enduring peace and justice for this planet. Jack Mendelsohn has long led the way as one who articulates this faith and embodies it in his actions. This book is a treasure and a tinderbox of hope for our global future.

The Reverend Scotty McLennan
January 2006

Introduction

Being Liberal in an Illiberal Age was first published more than forty years ago. In the midst of the civil rights era, the country was also coping with the loss of President John F. Kennedy and facing the growing divisiveness of the war in Vietnam. Parts of the book were updated as late as 1985, when Ronald Reagan was one year into his second term. But the concerns of the book, liberalism and liberal religion, have never been more seriously challenged than they are today, in post–September 11, post–Patriot Act America.

If we ever needed a wake-up call to our better democratic nature, we need it now. The natural liberal bent is to want people to live, not die, for their beliefs, but both liberals and moderate conservatives are now the objects of extreme hostility from the radical right, both in religion and politics.

The dawning years of the twenty-first century have been a disaster for liberal religious values. After September 11, there seemed to be no way to stem the tide of vengeance. The terrorist attacks provided an emotional justification for an administration already committed to a neo-conservative ideology, emboldened by an evangelical and born-again brand of fundamentalist Christianity, and allied to the very military-corporate complex President Eisenhower warned against in his farewell address. Liberal values, religious and secular, were eclipsed by the shock and awe of the war in Iraq. Our leaders played on our fears instead of our ideals with false claims of weapons of mass destruction and collusion with terrorists.

Liberal values were swept aside by deliberate budget policies that reward those with the most wealth with yet more, by an assault on seventy years of hard-won social programs, a vast national spying network and torture endorsed by our Justice Department, a denial of the constitutional wall of separation between church and state, and assaults on the scientific community with the promotion of "faith" concepts of creation and conception.

We live in a time in which prevarication, corruption, and cronyism have raised serious questions about the kind of lone superpower the United States is becoming. It's easy to despair in today's illiberal age, but instead, I call on religious liberals to relish the challenge and opportunity of these days. Liberal values, after all, are as basic as the belief that human beings are capable of respectful, fair, and honorable behavior. Let us hold on to the promise of our liberal religious heritage to chart new courses, buoyed by a new enthusiasm for our approach to satisfying the spiritual hunger of our troubled times.

Liberal religion asks, how should we live, while we live? What uses shall we make of our free will? These are bedrock questions. In answering them, it matters profoundly that we put our faith into action and make deliberate choices about our loyalties and loves.

I made my fundamental choice long ago. I wanted freedom. Freedom to think, express, question, examine, grow, and change. But freedom without a firm foundation of faith in action and a sense of history is fragile. I anchored my faith in the great legacy of the liberal spirit and its values of human rights for all people, equal opportunity, public education, democracy, a clean environment, reproductive freedom, and equity in our economic system.

I knew from the beginning that I did not want to go it alone. I wanted to be rooted in an open-minded religious community, to be part of a spiritual circle of approving and encouraging eyes, to savor the world and to help save it. I craved the company of others

—in worship, celebration, fellowship, study, service, spiritual discipline, and social action. I found this in the Unitarian Universalist movement and in each of the congregations I have been privileged to serve.

As a Unitarian Universalist, I dedicate my life to the creative religious behavior of seeking persons who learn to live in close touch with their times, who refuse to be spiritually numbed by its problems, and who undertake to resolve them, both within themselves and in their activities in the world.

To liberals, every age is illiberal. Forget perfection; that's not the issue. Remember instead the failings, shortcomings, repressions, persecutions, egocentricities, and hypocrisies in the human condition. They are unfailingly present, but so, too, is the struggle against them and the small successes. Remember them as well. Our present state at any moment can certainly be oppressive, but it need not be defeating. Our capacity for folly is very strong, but so, too, is our capacity, as Lewis Thomas once taught us, to "talk to each other, figure out the world, be useful, and above all, keep an eye out for affection."

I am a liberal because I want to take my stand with the liberal legacy, a spirit that pulls for the positive possibilities in the human endowment. I am a Unitarian Universalist because it is a religion that zestfully celebrates reason as the uniquely human ability to know ourselves and to transcend ourselves. It is the task of reason in this wider sense to point our way toward what ought to be. Through reason we come to care for ideals, for the arts of logical distinction and cultivated judgment. Through reason, we understand the meaning of giving and the importance of having a self to give. We see that the struggle for the lives of others is as fundamental as the struggle for personal survival. The self is private, personal, and precious, but it is not isolated from other selves. It is wholly unique, but it only shares, not commands, the universe.

Our garlanding of reason does not ignore faith. Theologian James Fowler has urged us to think of faith as a verb, not a noun. We faith together as a fundamental style of life, a way of relating to self, to others, to power, to boundaries such as death and finitude, and to sources of being, value, and meaning. We participate in common "faithing" in our Unitarian Universalist religious communities.

By faith, we relate ourselves to creation, not by having dominion but as participants in a symbiotic, wondrous, coherent body of connected life. By faith, we relate to others in caring, not possessing ways. By faith, we practice a strong sense of religious community, not to shut ourselves in or others out, but to make us better people, to rekindle our joy and zest in living.

By faith, we are part of a church that is not merely a structure but a center of sanity and inspiration in a deranged world; that is not merely a place of private cultivation and retreat but a temple for revitalizing our beleaguered values; a place that stands as a symbol of humans aspiring together, tracking truth together, and demanding social justice together; a place that has within it the exuberance of play, the blessings of shared celebration, and a symmetry with life's rhythms.

By faith, we nurture our children and youth so that they will not be mirrors of ourselves. Though they should fully know where we stand and may learn from us our better traits, we guarantee them their freedom to discover, develop, and live their own values.

By faith, we strive to become more centered, more spontaneous, more genuine, more constant persons. But by faith, we strive also not to be so focused on ourselves that we turn from the struggles against injustice and oppression.

By faith, we aspire to love life but to hold it loosely, knowing that we must die, knowing that we must constantly strike a balance between what we desire and what we can do, that it is only in imaginary worlds that we can do whatever we please or have whatever we want, that often we must choose and act among confounding paradoxes and ambiguities. By faith, we strive to savor even our small successes as experiences of liberation.

Human nature and its champion, liberalism, suffer often from a wretched press. Those who would like nothing better than to control our lives try constantly to fasten on us their pet pieties.

These will be fatal days for the liberal spirit if today's generation is without stalwarts who can do the hard work of groping for solutions, as halting and imperfect as they may be. Unitarian Universalism provides not an exclusive but a special and inclusive place for such stalwarts. These many years of laboring in its vineyards have both chastened and deepened the pride I take in calling it the religion of my heart and mind.

Now is always the best time to redefine, revitalize, and reconnect the liberal spirit to the human future.

The Reverend Jack Mendelsohn
January 2006

A Way of Walking and
Acting in the World

Human life is a struggle—against frustration, ignorance, suffering, evil, the maddening inertia of things in general; but it is also a struggle for something which our experience tells us can be achieved in some measure.

JULIAN HUXLEY

The more we try to say precisely what is in our hearts, the more we find that we are speaking for multitudes of strangers the world over. The deeper we get down to our own fundamentals, the more deeply we represent those of other people. Like all human beings, I live on borrowed time. I never know when my time will run out, but I do know that it will run out. I have no way of knowing what tragedies will befall me at the next step, the next ring of the telephone, the next rising of the sun. My notion of spiritual fulfillment is learning how to accept this fate with a ringing affirmation of all that makes life worth living.

The liberal spirit is my inspiration to be a creative, cooperative human being, in spite of the fact that life may crush me at any moment and death may blot me out. As a skeptic about such matters, I cannot comfort myself with supernatural promises. I know that human existence contains irreducible elements of tragedy and incompleteness. I know that I can never really comprehend the totality of things. I am finite. For me the fundamental question of life is not why but how. How shall I live while I live? This is the bedrock question. In answering it, it matters very much what I believe. As we read in the Apocryphal book called *Ecclesiasticus*:

> Accept no person against thine own soul,
> And let no reverence for anyone cause thee to fall.
> But let the counsel of thine own heart stand:
> For there is none more faithful unto thee than it.
> For our minds are sometimes wont to bring us tidings,
> More than seven watchmen, that sit above in a high tower.

It takes strong girders of conviction to keep the counsels of thine own liberal-spirited heart standing. Heinrich Heine, the German poet, was gazing with a friend at the cathedral in Amiens.

Asked the friend: "Tell me, Heinrich, why can't people build piles like this any more?"

Answered Heine: "My dear friend, in those days people had convictions. We moderns have opinions. And it takes more than opinions to build a Gothic cathedral."

I think of this exchange when I dwell on the massive attacks directed against the modern age, and its alleged inspiration, liberalism, usually uttered, in William F. Buckley, Jr., fashion, with a scornful curl of the lip.

Modernity's ambiguity, confusion, and sheer madness are enough to send the dazed rushing pell-mell toward certainty and direction. The limitless reaches of science and reason collapse into uncertainty and anxiety. "Where, oh where, is our center?" is a bleat of our times. The open mind? Why, it turns out to be nothing but a sieve. Even the most respected scientists say so. Take Niels Bohr's "Every sentence that I utter should be regarded by you not as an assertion but as a question." And Jacob Bronowski's "There is no absolute knowledge. . . . All information is imperfect." Modernity's only certainty is everlasting uncertainty. All that was thought to be solid dissolves in the air, adding to the pollution.

A generation hungering for certainties is like a vacuum. It

sucks in evangelists of reactionary nostrums bearing conservative labels. Thus we are well launched into an era of regressive politics and regressive religion, in which the liberal spirit is at the head of a line of perceived evils, followed in no particular order by abortion, welfare, food stamps, affirmative action, sex education, the United Nations, aid to the Third World, disarmament, Soviet expansionism, and on and on.

What exactly is this satanic liberalism? To me, and by and large to history, it is a way of walking and acting in the world. It means celebrating and practicing the importance of persons: their inherent freedom to think, speak, associate, hear, read, see, and learn; not perfect freedom, but responsible freedom, become manifest in the particulars of our lives. It means warmly embracing political democracy and constitutional, compassionate government. Among its meanings are social justice, popular education, equal opportunity and access, peaceful resolution of conflict, broad tolerance of diversity, the scientific spirit of inquiry, a rational outlook, a relativistic philosophy, and ethicosocial religion.

In my life, the liberal spirit is wholistic. It informs my being in all of its dimensions—spiritual, political, social, private and public. I recognize, with appreciation and respect, that this is not a universal condition. There are numerous religious liberals who are conservative in their politics and religious conservatives who are liberal in their politics.

I claim no heavenly sanction for my all-embracing liberal way of walking in life's paths. Still, those who join me in trying to practice it are apt to be puzzled by the fervor with which it is smitten hip and thigh, not just by partisans of the right, but of the left as well.

Disparagement of liberalism from the right is normal and seemingly eternal. But today, the liberal spirit is exuberantly despised by many on the left. Black, feminist, and Third World liberationists, and many peace activists, often have that special Buckley-like curl to their lips when they pronounce the word *liberal*. Yet, as I shall point out, *liberation* and *liberal* come from the same Latin root. They are kin.

A solemn look back to Martin Luther King, Jr., may be instructive. Dr. King was steeped in liberalism. Liberals loved him when he spoke for nonviolence in Montgomery. Liberals loved him when he wrote his stirring letter from the Birmingham jail, where he was incarcerated for opposing Bull Connor's police dogs and fire hoses with freedom songs. Liberals loved him at the Lincoln Memorial in 1963 when he linked his dream and the dream of black people with the liberal dream.

But how quickly frightened liberals deserted him when, at Riverside Church in 1963, he said that the struggle for justice at home and for an end to the war in Vietnam were one and the same. Liberal leaders raced to the television cameras and into print to accuse him of jeopardizing the civil rights movement by linking the two issues. We can only guess his thoughts when many of those same keepers of the liberal flame finally came around to saying what he had said three years earlier.

Liber, with whom both *liberal* and *liberation* are connected, was the Roman god of fertility and wine. It was natural, therefore, that *liberal* came to be applied to what was generous and open, to the unrestricted and unfettered, not bound by established mores to the orthodox and formal. Nor was it unnatural, in the eyes of certain respectables to whom the suggestion of a pregnant universe was distasteful if not downright threatening, that *liberal* evoked the licentious and chaotic. This we can understand. More difficult to understand are liberationists whose derision concentrates on liberalism rather than on reaction. Kinship struggles are often nasty.

To a certain extent, anti-liberal diatribes are a fashionable expression of human meanness and frustration. We all have a scurvy streak in us that we are bound to express. Now it is open season on liberals, who frequently respond by splenetically attacking one another.

Frustrations among liberationists are very real. They have to be vented somewhere. So why not on liberals, currently a pretty defenseless lot? In addition, the cyclicity of liberalism is an old story. Liberalism, religious and political, flowers, gets locked into transient programs, trends, parties, and tactics and withers, only to flower again. During its withering periods, reaction always takes heart, which is certainly true today, and liberals enter into a kind of choleric introspection. Nor is there anything historically original about those of more radical bent snapping at liberals for being mere reformers, when root-and-branch revolution is what is obviously needed. This too is an old story.

The trouble with too many liberals, according to radicalized blacks, women, youth, gays, and peace activists, is their complacent spirit. Yes, they have a decent concern for social change. But where is the passion? Where is the sense of their own oppression? Buried in middle-class standards. That's where it is. Tucked into the benefits that infuriatingly unjust social structures have bestowed upon them. Yes, they would like to share these benefits with the less fortunate, those who have been locked out and denied access, but at little or no cost to themselves and their children.

The evils of society burn a hole in the soul, say liberationists. We have a gut reaction, a kind of upset that can never be adequately expressed by the liberal's "decent concern."

How is this gulf to be bridged? I speak as a liberal in search of redemption and reconstruction—one whose soul is full of holes burned by the evils of society. If liberalism is to arise from whatever malaise withers it, if it is to reach out, it must be a humbled, radicalized, stretched, and shriven liberalism. It must be a liberalism with a monumental abhorrence of hypocrisy and cant. It must be a liberalism that knows, not just a decent concern for oppression, but a personal experience of it and a profound sense of agony and outrage. In brief, it must be a liberalism ecstatic enough and disciplined enough to celebrate, demand, organize, institutionalize, suffer for, and exult over profound social and individual change.

I speak then for a transformed liberalism. Scavenging for hope in this task does not mean donning "conservative" clothes and calling oneself a neoliberal. As for the self-styled conservatives of this age, typically they are nursers of their own resentments and defenders of their own interests.

On the other hand, there is no genuinely effective radical movement.

That leaves liberalism, however disarrayed and weary its troops, among whom there is a distressing loss of heart. But this is characteristic of liberalism, which is experiencing, as before, the agony of its success. Years ago, pioneers like Jane Addams and John Dewey helped launch a liberalism that was high on mental freedom and social compassion. They succeeded. Millions of people were introduced to new appreciations of economic equity and civic participation. The trouble with liberalism is that once it's successful as it has been in so many realms—from women's rights to minority rights, from universal public education to protection of the environment, from progressive taxation to Medicaid— liberals don't know what to do. All of this is accomplished, yet illiberalism flourishes. What should liberals do, not just to beat back reactionary assaults, but to gird for new positive thrusts?

Here are some possible revisions of the liberal idea, which once again might make it, in new shapes and forms, a powerful social force.

First there is the advocacy of a new theory of intellect, a new mode of perception, a new way of acting. Liberalism has always been right in its devotion to reason. But reason has been interpreted too narrowly for the present age. We assume that what we call reality exhausts reality, that what we call the human story is the real human story, and that our Western symbols are universally binding to all humanity. Shall we try to persuade, or even force, all of earth's men and women to become like us? Do North American mind-sets and world views represent the best of what the world is capable of? Will human value truly be advanced if North Americans make over the entire planet in their present image?

What liberals also need is an infusion of intelligent subjectivity, which is not a reaction against reason but an extension of reason, a way of looking at reality that snatches reason from the hands of textbook scientists, logicians, and technologists. What is needed is an expanded consciousness, capable of taking more seriously the data for reflection and reverence that come from feelings, instincts, insights—in short, from the whole realm of creative imagination. We keep trying to live like scientists, when in fact most of the important decisions we make—choosing a spouse, changing a job—are not scientific at all. And because we try to live like scientists, many in the world become convinced that we are spiritually underdeveloped and lacking in soul.

Liberals who permit new forms of consciousness to express themselves may get on the move again and be threatened by new successes. Wouldn't that be something?

A reminder is in order. Respecting ambiguity and distrusting absolutes is not bad. Questioning received opinion and the authority of doctrines that defy reason is a reassuring means of perceiving that irrationalism underlies many seductive "certainties" peddled by slick, thriving hucksters. The liberal spirit takes the questions of the age seriously and doesn't try to answer unasked or wasteful questions. It accepts our human finiteness and fallibility and rejects unrelenting certitude. This emphasis on openness (humility?), far from being like a sieve, can be a robust listening to other possibilities, as well as a shield against salvationist nostrums and premature closures.

Where, then, is the solid ground on which liberals plant their feet? How about a rich menu of values, goals, priorities, and agendas? There is a special kind of derision reserved for these "abstractions." But how impalpable are they really? Not at all, if you stop to think about how most of us try to live our lives. Values, goals, priorities, and agendas are the very stuff of the weal and woe of life. Bless the liberal spirit for beckoning us to treat the stuff with intense seriousness and saving humor.

The effectiveness is uneven, to be sure, but the liberal spirit helps its devotees to risk experiencing the tangles and riddles of modern life, free from blanched fevers where truth is never gray. The raw reality is that we live and die in the embrace of imperfection and relative judgments. Returning the embrace seems a reasonable faith by which to live.

Despite these earned hallelujas, liberalism faces the waning of the century with tired blood. It is so pummeled that many are diagnosing brain death. The heart still beats, diagnosticians say, and the outer extremities still respond in Pavlovian fashion to external stimuli. Some, whose wish is parent to the thought, claim that liberalism's death certificate and autopsy are at hand. They already know what the findings will be: death by hyper-confusion. Alas, a massive vascular accident induced by overextended uncertainty. Too much indulgence in paradoxes and ambiguities.

Others surmise that the overriding affliction of liberals is elitism: walling themselves into discrete, precious enclaves—each absorbed by some special cause, some unique set of ideas to play with. Requirements for admission can be seen as quite cliquish. Most people rebel against a steady diet of critical intellect. They hunger for transcendent nourishment and are frustrated by too much search and too little discovery. Frustration in turn will extend an uncritical welcome to almost any kind of metaphysical mooring, possibly something caring and sensitive, often commercial gimmickry, and in too many instances cruel claptrap. Yet no amount of jeering and lecturing will discourage those who feel driven to take the gamble.

It is liberals who take a risk by denying the extreme spiritual discomfort of openness without commitment. Doubt is important in faith, but only if it is a means of keeping faith activated and enlivened. Doubt as an end in itself is deadly. There is nothing liberal about indifference to the human need for spiritual direction. To think so is to betray ignorance of the human condition.

We need to remind the world of the affirmations of liberalism if we expect it to listen to liberalism's complaints about quacks and rascals. The need for centering points in a careening world is real and rightful. Groundedness and rootedness are positives, not negatives. They are the crux of any transforming ministry to life. Liberals take notice. If we view liberalism as, in D.H. Lawrence's words, "an uprooted tree, with its roots in the air" (letter to the Reverend Robert Reid), nothing less than strenuous affirmation will supplant it. To say that we do not have the whole truth is not to say that we have no truth. Like Saint Paul, we see through a glass darkly, but we do see. Openness without wholeness and commitment is a clanging cymbal.

I was grateful when there came an invitation to share with a gathering of midwestern religious liberals the articles of liberal faith undergirding my social activism. It was an exciting task of self-examination and distillation—elementary and elemental. In the end I described four liberal/liberating convictions by which I live.

1. I am life that wills to live in the midst of life that wills to live.
2. Separating the essential from the nonessential is what I call being spiritual.
3. Power, ethically understood, is the ability to achieve moral purpose.
4. Nothing is settled; balance is blessedness.

Nietzsche wrote: "We are unknown, we knowers, to ourselves. . . . Of necessity we remain strangers to ourselves, we understand ourselves not, in our selves we are bound to be mistaken" (*Thus Spake Zarathustra*).

I respect the wisdom in this. But, as with so much of Nietzsche, it is overstated. I know myself imperfectly, but I am no complete stranger to myself and to what makes me tick. I am not "bound to be mistaken" in what I believe that I believe.

In addition to being a person, spouse, parent, and grandparent, I am a preacher, counselor, teacher, and would-be prophet. The sheer mess of human conditions that cry out for deliverance —from poverty, oppression, and bondage—appalls me. I experience human suffering and degradation as my own pain. I don't just read about them and think, Isn't that terrible? As a responsible advocate of human life and dignity, I hurt, and the hurt grips me at the roots of my being.

I also experience life as grace-filled wonder. Statistically, the possibility of any of us being here is so infinitesimal that the mere fact of our existence is confounding. As E.B. White put it in the *New Yorker*:

If the world were merely seductive, that would be easy. If it were merely challenging, that would be no problem. But I arise in the morning, torn between a desire to improve (or save) the world, and a desire to enjoy (or savor) the world. This makes it hard to plan the day.

As for the cosmic meanings of human life, I am content with a deep and abiding modesty. I simply do not know. But as for the finite meanings of human life, experienced in dazzlement and deliverance, in rights and repression, in surprise and struggle, in living and dying, I have no uncertainties. These meanings are real. They matter. I cannot and will not abdicate the quest for finite human fulfillment. If, cosmically speaking, human life is a trip to nowhere, so be it. I will not live my life, precious gift that it is, according to that rubric.

So, there is a special joy in sharing what sustains, directs, chastens, and validates my bittersweet journey along the boundaries of such a liberal faith

Life as a Gift

I am life that wills to live in the midst of life that wills to live. My life is a gift, a grace, if you wish. I had nothing to do with planning, creating, or initially shaping it. With my gift of life comes a unique endowment—human consciousness: a drive not only to be, but to be fulfilled. As I grew and developed, it was impressed upon me that my will to live and to be fulfilled existed in the midst of other wills to live and to be fulfilled. I learned that I could look out from within myself and see a life view, a world view. How then might I best express gratitude for my own gift of life? By reverencing not only my own will to live and to be fulfilled, but that of others. How could I do this? By sympathy, obviously. By self-development. By discipline. By encounter. By associated effort. We do not live alone. We live together. We depend on one another. To forget that is to become spiritually lost, like fiery particles flung off from the solar system and quenched meaninglessly in outer space.

For me, the great teacher of this spiritual and ethical affirmation of the gift of life is Albert Schweitzer, an exemplar of what I think is liberalism at its best, namely that progress does not come easily or automatically. Quite the contrary. His view of human beings (including himself, of course) was pessimistic. It was his willing, hoping, and acting that were optimistic. It is the same for me. I shut my eyes to none of human nature's aberrations. I do not believe that human reason is an all-sufficient force for good. My liberal faith is anchored in our membership in one another and in a consciously embraced ethical spirit generated by this truth.

Being Spiritual

Separating the essential from the nonessential is what I call being spiritual.

I found this phrase, years ago, floating in one of Corita Kent's gossamer paintings. It has since hung on my study wall, where I can contemplate it each morning.

There has never been, nor will there ever be, enough time or opportunity to learn everything, to do everything, or care even-handedly about everything. We can never be completely satisfied or satisfiable, adjusted or adjustable. We continually run out of energy, ability, and courage. We are hurtable. The temptation is ever upon us to exercise influence we have not earned and do not possess.

To be spiritual, for me, means knowing all of this and still offering up thanks for the privilege of being what we are. There is in us the stuff out of which new, affirming experiences are fashioned. So build we up the human beings that we are.

"Love the moment," says Corita Kent, "and the energy . . . will spread beyond all boundaries.

"Flowers grow out of dark moments.

"Your each moment is vital because it affects the whole.

"Live in the dark moment.

"Life is a succession of moments; to live each one is to succeed."

So, it is not essential to me to set precise meanings to the word

God. I know that only by living my limited moments will I grope toward truths about what God may be and what we are.

That's why I worry about dying, but not about death. Before I was born I knew nothing about life, and it certainly didn't worry me then. Death may be yet another state of being, or it may be a nonstate of nonbeing. I cannot know. Why should it worry me any more than life did before I was born?

But dying is an experience, an act in which I will be the central participant. It is essential to my spirituality to meditate upon that and to prepare for it as best I can, to think through the possible scenarios.

Like Henry David Thoreau, "I wish to learn what life has to teach, and not, when I come to die, discover that I have not lived." I want to immerse myself in the streams of intimacy and history. I want to live in this death-oriented world without letting death have power over me. I want to live in the fullest possible awareness of a true belonging, not just to those who are nearest and dearest to me, but to the times in which I live—the causes, emergencies, issues, desperations, and hopes.

Power and Moral Purpose

Power, ethically understood, is the ability to achieve moral purpose.

A crucial dimension of the gift of life and of its will to live in the midst of life that wills to live is the use of power. A liberal (and liberating) faith, in both its personal and communal forms, must come to terms with the realities of power. Social action is the exercise of power. Ethical social action is the exercise of power for implementing the demands of justice, equity, and love.

Power is two-dimensional. One dimension is *an* expression of ultimate reality, or, as many would say, of God's law and love. The other dimension is the exercise of human freedom. Understanding power as ultimate reality, or as God's law and love, means that in exercising it one is compelled by the ethical necessities of being fully human: to seek human community in the fulfillment of interdependent spiritual destinies, of life that wills to live in the midst of life that wills to live. Power understood as human freedom is our response to the possibilities in creation, which are both personal and institutional.

Power, ethically understood, is the ability to achieve moral purpose. It is the capacity, inherent in our being, "to bring good tidings to the afflicted; . . . to bind up the broken-hearted, to proclaim liberty to the captives, . . . to comfort all who mourn" (Isaiah 61:1–2).

The idea of power and the exercise of power must never be viewed as alien to the liberal spirit. Power is a basic dimension of being and a basic dimension of the personal and institutional liberal life. It is both desirable and necessary in implementing the demands of love and justice.

Martin Luther King, Jr., taught that "one of the greatest problems of history is that the concepts of love and power are usually contrasted as polar opposites. Love is identified with a resignation of power and power with a denial of love. . . . What is needed is a realization that power without love is reckless and abusive and that love without power is sentimental and anemic. Power at its best is love implementing the demands of justice. Justice at its best is love correcting everything that stands against love" (*Where Do We Go From Here?*).

These words, to me, are a veritable manifesto for an empowered liberalism. I say, Amen!

As a Team

Nothing is settled; balance is blessedness.

If I had to give a six-word definition of normative liberalism, this would be it. Take, for example, these two familiar areas of experience: innovation and tradition, and spiritual nurture and public action.

Innovation and Tradition.
In the Book of Acts (17:21) there is a description of those who

hung around the Areopagus in Athens as "people who spent their time in nothing except telling and hearing something new." This is an impression we liberals frequently give. Trendy. Zealots of the latest. Innovators. Prizers of telling and hearing the new (as well we should be). But we also have a magnificent history, bequeathed to us by the labors and sufferings of forebears, known and unknown: thinkers, confessors, apostles, prophets, and martyrs. We are a rooted people, we liberals, who should be everlastingly respectful and proud of our tradition and inheritance.

Many of the problems of our common life in the liberal spirit rise from losing our sense of innovation or tradition. We get into trouble when we slip into an idolatry of only one. It is essential to our genius to love the making of new wine, but it is also essential to our genius to savor the mature, full-bodied wine of our heritage.

Nothing is settled; balance is blessedness.

Spiritual Nurture and Public Action.
Inward and outward; personal growth and social witness. Once again, nothing is settled; balance is blessedness. We have swung between these "birches" for as long as our history runneth. Emerson put it this way: "These wonderful horses need to be driven by fine hands" ("Society and Solitude").

The liberal spirit is for healing our ever-battered souls: in solitude, in touching intimacies, in deep, searching disciplines. But we are in the world and must act in the world—as free individuals and as community persons. Nothing is finally settled by that either. We often act in hollowness. Spiritual preparation, private and communal, for acting in the world is crucial. Everything that has to do with our common humanity and how it is nourished is important. Everything that stretches from self to society and from society to self is important. These wonderful horses need to be driven, as a team, with fine hands. Balance is blessedness.

These days it is easy to despair of liberalism's weaknesses, so it is of consequence to be aware of our present and potential strengths.

One of these is our enduring function of living on the boundaries —between mind and body, the internal and the external, freedom and necessity, individual and community.

We have never had a better opportunity to live not as one-side-or-the-other partisans of left brain-right brain, mysticism-empiricism, intuitive-rational, piety-society, nurture-nature, but as agile boundary-dwellers, at home on both sides of the borders: pilgrims of the reconciliations that must come if the human race is to survive.

As one familiar with significant voluntary associations of liberal bent, I know how rich the opportunities are for such valuing communities—as relatively stable, preventive arrangements against personal and social pathology and as centers for the generation of liberating change.

We liberals are members of a historic movement with accrued status and moral authority to stand as a counterpoint to the death of moral goodness. We who speak the language of the liberal spirit and live out of its bosom can be key figures in the struggle both to save and to savor the world. If this sounds inflated, remember that Daedalus's warning to his son Icarus was not just against flying too high. It was also against flying too low.

Security

I am not a liberal because it gives me security. No one should try the liberal spirit looking for that result. What liberalism appeals to in me is what Carl Sandburg, in "Man the Moon Shooter," described as the "moon shooter" part of our nature:

> The shapes of change
> ai ai they take their time
> asking what the dawn asks
> giving the answers evening gives
> till tomorrow moves in
> saying to . . . the moon shooter

'Now I am here—now read me—
give me a name.'

We humans, in Sandburg's eyes, are moon shooters: restless, roving, inquisitive creatures, ever striving for unknown futures. There is no real stopping place, no status quo. There are always the next shapes of change to come.

It was Christmas Day, 1983, late afternoon. Our family, twelve in number, four generations, was in the midst of a high-decibel, high-calorie holiday dinner, when the phone rang. It was Jesse Jackson. "Jack," he said, "a Merry Christmas to you and Joan and the family."

"Same to you, Jesse, and to Jacqueline, and all your kids."

"Jack, I want you to go to Syria with me, to get Lieutenant Robert Goodman and bring him home."

"When do you plan to leave, Jesse?"

"Probably on Wednesday, three days from now. The Syrians say we can see Goodman and that Assad will talk with us. They say they aren't going to let him go, but I think we can get him. I want you with me."

"Jesse, let me talk it over with my family, and I'll get back to you."

The family talked. They were accustomed to the "moon shooter" nature of my relationship with Jesse Jackson. With their blessing, I flew off to Damascus on December 29, 1983, as a member of the Jackson mission. The rest is history. We brought Lieutenant Goodman home. Indeed, there are always the next shapes of change to come.

But what about rest for the weary soul? Moon shooting is exciting. But we are also creatures in need of tranquility. What place is there for inner quiet and peace? We do need the thrill of change, of movement, but we also need dependable things, reliable things, steady things, things that stand fast while we think our way through the enigmas, puzzles, and horrors of a swiftly changing world.

Sandburg raises an ancient problem. We are indeed moon shooters, but we also long for solid ground beneath our feet. Where will we find that solid ground? In what thoughts, what beliefs, what faiths? In the midst of change, on what can we depend?

Robert Frost warmed to these questions in his narrative poem "The Star-Splitter," which tells the story of Brad McLaughlin, described by Frost as a "Hugger-mugger" New Hampshire farmer.

> He burned his house down for the fire insurance
> And spent the proceeds on a telescope
> To satisfy a life-long curiosity
> About our place among the infinities.

At first, Frost tells us, there was some mean laughter, but soon the townsfolk began to reflect:

> If one by one we counted people out
> For the least sin, it wouldn't take us long
> To get so we had no one left to live with,
> For to be social is to be forgiving.

So, Brad McLaughlin bought his telescope and took a job as ticket agent for the old Concord railroad, a job that gave him leisure for stargazing. He and his friend, the narrator, spent countless hours in the evening looking up "the brass barrel, velvet black inside, at a star quaking in the other end."

> We've looked and looked, but after all where are we?
> Do we know any better where we stand,
> And how it stands between the night tonight
> And (someone) with a smoky lantern chimney?
> How different from the way it ever stood?

Frost has pondered the questions about security and raised some new ones about serenity. Is it abnormal to want serenity? Can we be moon shooters and still be serene? Can we find serenity in the stars or in anything outside our own being? If we cannot find serenity in the stars, can we find it in what the stars help us to learn about ourselves?

Let's go back again to that solid ground beneath our feet. In a spiritual sense, where are we likely to find it? By leaps of irrationality? In unquestioning obedience? Does this universe make life easier for us if we subscribe to the right creed, follow the right leader, or pledge the right allegiance? We must be morally myopic to think it is that kind of universe! Where then is security? Where is the solid ground? If we want an answer, a strong answer, one that does not try to blink the facts or sentimentalize the realities, we can hardly do better than the tough thoughts of the tender-spirited Emerson: "Nothing is secure but life, transition, the energizing spirit. No love can be bound by oath or covenant to secure it against a higher love. No truth so sublime but it may be trivial tomorrow in the light of new thoughts. People wish to be settled; only in so far as they are unsettled is there any hope." And then Emerson startles us with a conjecture that we never rise so high as when we know not whither we are going.

Obviously Emerson offers us little in the way of lulling assurance. If we never rise so high as when we know not whither we are going, most of us would have little trouble soaring free into the stratosphere. Perhaps there is more to this than first meets the eye. Possibly it is in just such a time as ours, when it is impossible to know exactly where we are going, that we are literally forced by our problems and challenges to rise to new heights of coping and achieving. Is it, after all, so important to know precisely where we are going, as long as we know the general direction in which we want to travel and the stronger, warmer companions we will need for the journey? What more should we ask than the solid reliance on the faith that somehow, because of the nature of what is required of us, we will respond and rise higher than we dreamed possible? If only a wiser, nobler humanity is equal to our present problems, then a wiser, nobler humanity we will be.

By no stretch of the imagination can this be called security. At least it is not the kind of security that makes us feel smug and safe from the barbs of life. "Nothing is secure," says Emerson, "but life, transition, and the energizing spirit." With this perspective, we achieve a larger and revitalized conception of liberal faith. If we would find solid ground beneath our feet, we must have courage enough to give up illusions of a protected life and accept our role as servants of life, agents of transition, and incarnations of the energizing spirit, subject to all the stresses and shocks of life, but confident and buoyant through them all. This is the liberal spirit at its greatest, not a petty search for protection or a pinched hope of piecemeal benevolence, but the wonderful adventure of life itself, as solemn as a world that is dying and as supple as a world that is waiting to be born, as expectant as souls who see clearly what is required of them and rise empowered to make and meet a better future. This kind of liberal spirit is solid ground, and when we have discovered it and made it our own, nothing can take it away.

What of serenity? We will not find it in tranquilizing sermons that are on the self-help shelves of bookstores. Many of the pulpit recitals and cozy, expensive seminars devoted to serenity and success are geared to those who seek an easy way and can afford it. There is no easy way. The road to serenity is as rigorous as any we will ever travel. Serenity comes not from escaping the realities of life, but from being in the midst of them. The best human beings have always been those who achieved serenity by taking upon themselves the pain, fear, suffering, cruel passions, and murky guilts of human inhumanity toward other humans. Whether we speak of a Catholic Mother Teresa, a Jewish Martin Buber, or a Unitarian Joseph Tuckerman, we know that this is the truth of the matter. No one comes by serenity cheaply. To gain it, we have to meet its requirements; we have to do the deeds and make the choices that bring serenity in their wake. For each of us, it means making, not just alone, but in the disciplined company of others, the difficult choices, the demanding choices.

It means wading into the river of history and accepting one's place in it. It means breaking bread at a common table of memories and aspirations, rejoicing in identification with causes, emergencies, movements, parties. As William Ernest Hocking put it in *The Coming World Civilization*: "Failure to accept responsibility, refusal to take a stand on vital issues, timid rejection . . . of the ties of a true belonging, these are denials of life—in effect they are deeds of death."

The greatest and most emboldening of blessings is the will to care enough about the times in which we live to know where and to what moral ends we want to put our efforts on the line. This is, in Hocking's words, "life with shape and character." No one can consciously choose the lower against the higher and know inner peace. Serenity is involvement with the unserene.

We began with two poets: one who speaks of us as moon shooters, and another who spins a yarn about a farmer who sought solace in an ill-gotten telescope. We found them raising profound questions about security and serenity. In each case, the answer came back: Look within and look around you! The tasks of finding solid ground, of making peace with oneself and one's times, are tasks in the midst of change, challenge, and conflict. If we break under the weight of our burdens, we break, isolated, from within. If we master life, that mastery also comes from within, but is connected. All of life is change, and we cannot escape it. We look for strength and peace, and where do we find them but in being useful, being whole, being warm members of the human family, of adding our weight to what is called for by the deep nature of life.

That's what the liberal spirit is about, has always been about.

A Human Being, No More or Less

> I came to see the damage that was done and the treasures
> that prevail.
>
> ADRIENNE RICH

Humans are "glorious and happy," according to William Ellery Channing, not by what they have, but by what they are. They can receive nothing better or nobler than "the unfolding of their own spiritual nature."

The liberal spirit's supreme gift to me was an introduction to the Unitarian Universalist religious community, where I found encouragement to unfold: the special joy of breaking out of the cocoon or of discovering a greater freedom in the exercise of my intelligence and in the growth of my experience of love, beauty, and justice.

Childhood is a quilt of many patches: sounds, smells, tears, playgrounds, back fences, anticipations. Mine was such a childhood, a compound of chance and purpose, marvel and misery. I remember with special warmth my maternal grandfather, Charles M. Torrey, of the Foxboro, Massachusetts, Torreys. He had been one of the early touring professional baseball players. It was he who guided my first nervous attempts at playing sandlot baseball. He gave me his very own cornet, battered and old, on which I learned the beginnings of the musical skills that eventually helped finance my college education.

I remember the summer, my twelfth, when I fastened a chinning bar on the back porch in the conviction that it would help to stretch my body to the more than six feet of height I so desperately desired. By the age of seventeen, the chinning bar long forgotten, I made it to six feet and three inches and stopped growing.

I remember the boyhood hours I spent poring over Uncle Lawrence Farwell's picture book of World War I. He had been an artilleryman in France, a feat I greatly admired. I nursed a morbid fear that there might never be another war in which I could perform valorous deeds. Such are the unpredictabilities of childhood! By the time we found ourselves in World War II, I was a confirmed pacifist, an ardent convert to nonviolence.

As I look back over the tender years, there is little that prophesied my eventual turn toward a Unitarian Universalist ministry, except that I was an avid reader. My room, to the dismay of my parents and, later, my grandparents, was forever strewn with books. At Christmas and birthdays there were only two kinds of gifts I really wanted: athletic equipment and books. As for religion, it was anything but a burden. None of my relatives pried into my religious thoughts, and I did very little prying of my own. My father, Jack Mendelsohn, Sr., born Jewish, was an uncomplicated person religiously and, like his father before him, nonobserving. Theology was about as pressing for him as witchcraft.

I worshipped my mother, Anna Melissa Torrey Mendelsohn, and was never given the opportunity to grow beyond a boy's craving for approval and affection. She was statuesque, red-headed, and very beautiful. Or so I remember. She was youthful. Even as a child, when anyone over twenty seemed ancient, I was deeply conscious of her youth. She played the piano professionally. That was how my father, then a music publisher, met her. She cooked wonderful soups and often held me in her lap. I needed her terribly and was painfully aware of it.

One day I ran home from school. I was six and a first grader in the old Morse School in Cambridge. The teacher left the room, and the children exploded into a chaos of screaming, jumping, and throwing erasers. Suddenly she was back, and I stood transfixed with eraser in hand. Enraged, she pulled me from the room and ordered me to stand alone in the hall until she was ready to deal with me. I was the only culprit she apprehended and humbled. Part of what I felt was fear, but a great part was outrage. In the face of massive injustice, I bolted from the corridor and ran home, where I knew there would be justice even though it would include punishment for my transgression. I was not disappointed. My mother deprived me of several privileges for a few days, but she also took me back to school, hand in hand, where she charmed and soothed the distraught teacher and returned me honorably to my peers.

This is the mother I remember. It was difficult for me to think of God as being other than a woman, like my mother.

Then life taught me something else.

I was eight and shared a room with my sister, Virginia, who was three years younger than I. One night I awoke in the darkness and peered into the hall where I caught a harrowing glimpse of my father helping my mother down the stairs. Her face was twisted with pain. It was the last time I saw her.

Years later I learned it was a miscarriage that took her to the hospital that night. My grandmother, Mary Spinney Torrey, came the next morning and an air of mystery hung on the house. The following night I awoke again and heard my grandmother and father whispering together. Soon they left, unaware that I was awake. But I knew what was happening. While my sister slept, I paced in the darkness of our parents' room, sobbing aloud, "She can't die. Oh, God, don't let her die!"

She did die, and at dawn my father and grandmother returned to tell us what I already knew. The cause of death, though it had no meaning for me at the time, was peritonitis, an abdominal inflammation. All that mattered to me was the loss of the most important person in the world. I was hurt and angry, desolate and resentful. For the first time in my life I had asked God for something. I had begged God for something! And God had turned and slapped me in the face, as I had seen some parents strike my playmates.

Since that moment religious questions have never been far from my thoughts. It may be a gift or a neurosis, but I am gripped with the habit of religious searching. It would be wrong, however, to give the impression of youthful zealotry or intense concentration.

Soon after my mother's death, my sister became a member of Aunt Mabel Farwell's household, and I went to live with my Torrey grandparents in Cambridge, Massachusetts. We were neighbors, just a few streets apart. My father, who had shifted from publishing music to selling furniture, took up residence in a New York City hotel. Though we saw him regularly, we were never again a united family.

My grandparents were quiet, steady, sober New Englanders. My grandfather had been a barnstorming baseball player in that pastime's pioneer years. Later, he had become a fireman and policeman in his native Foxboro, where my mother was laid to rest among her Torrey forebears. When I joined their household, my grandfather had long been a minor functionary with the Elliott Addressing Machine Company in Cambridge. My grandmother, who in her younger days was a solo whistler on the church and lodge circuit in Washington County, Maine, cooked, mended, busied herself about the house, and looked after me with untiring solicitude. The two of them played dominoes almost every night of the years I lived with them. They encouraged me to study, to play, and to bring my friends home. Athletic skills became a passion for me, equaled only by my determination to be a top student. I gravitated to friends who felt the same.

My grandparents and the Farwells were unenthusiastically associated with a neighborhood church, Pilgrim Congregational, a center of conservative, evangelical Christianity. Because God was a paradox to me, I became the most ardent and faithful churchgoer of the family. The minister, the Reverend Stanley Addison, kind and careworn, whose preaching voice always sounded tearful, had officiated at my mother's funeral and was keenly con-

cerned about the welfare of my soul. The Sunday school superin-
tendent, Dr. Arthur Miles, an austere, elderly dentist, believed in
the fire of hell and was determined to guide me in another direction. From the beginning, I was both a protégé and a problem
child. Our relationship developed steadily but never smoothly.

In the sense that I was determined to ask Why and How do
you know, I suppose my religious future was set the night my
mother died, but it would be years before I recognized it. If religion was to make sense to me, it had to provide room for my in-
quisitiveness and rebellion. Somehow it had to encompass the
anguish and bewilderment I felt at God's failure to save my
mother. It had to be wide enough to let me ask whether God was
a demon, or whether God existed at all.

I expected to find answers in church, where the talk was inter-
minably of God, Jesus, prayer, and salvation. I listened and grew
confused and impudent. I tried to pray. I listened hard for God's
voice. I wanted to feel Jesus's arms about me. I prayed and had the
increasingly embarrassed feeling that no one was listening. If God
possessed a voice, it was strangely silent in my presence. The more
I thought about the Jesus who was being revealed to me in my religious education, the more unappealing and unreal he became.

What my religious tutors failed to realize was that a spell of
dissent was upon me like a divine discontent. It was not about
meek acceptance and a sense of sin that I wished to hear. I wanted
to be challenged and shaken. I wanted my spirit to be given something to strive for. I wanted to know why the world could be at
once wondrous and ugly. I wanted to know why I had both laughter and pain. If God had created me, I wanted to know who had
created God. Instead, I was backed into a corner and was implored
to surrender my soul to the Lord and Savior.

I stayed with the neighborhood church until I went to college
and lived much of my social life under its care. I knew from the
time I was twelve that I could never be a Christian as the word was
interpreted there, but as a teenager I sang in the adult choir, as a
high school senior I taught a Sunday school class of ten-year-old

boys, and I rarely missed a Sunday evening Christian Endeavor meeting for youth. These Pilgrim Congregational people were my friends, my familiars, my community, and though they trembled for my soul on grounds I considered nonsensical, I respected their sincerity and was grateful for their affection.

Such religion as I possess was born of conflict and has been, in its development, a struggle *against* resentment of a wound inflicted upon me when I was unable to defend myself and *for* a positive, constructive, unfettered spiritual freedom. In college there were added dimensions of an awakened social conscience and a desire to commit my life to the service of others. The open-mindedness of classicism, the probing of philosophy, the measuring of science, and the eclecticism of anthropology impressed upon me the endless diversity of human spiritual searchings. A firm decision against religious sectarianism was inevitable. I have sought a spiritual life that offers not surrender and salvation but, in Albert Camus's words, "love of life in spite of life." I have striven to accept flaws and to find things to live for that transcend and conquer them.

Faith, Admiration and Sympathy

For a time I was in a genuine dilemma about a career. After graduating from college, I spent three years testing the waters, first in the business world, then as a high school teacher and coach. I enjoyed both, gained confidence, and even accumulated savings. But all this time there was an underlying itch for the ministry. My philosophical views were radically at odds with traditional theology, yet I felt a deep affection for the *community* of the church, as I had experienced it. I kept thinking about what a profoundly useful vehicle it was, potentially, for moral improvement and social witness. The ministry, it seemed, offered one of the most rewarding and constructive careers to one whose mind responded enthusiastically to religious questions and who wanted, as I did, to cultivate skills in education, human relations, and the leadership of groups banded together to seek spiritual fortification, moral encouragement, and ethical effectiveness.

The passing years have only confirmed my early surmises about the ministry's possibilities. H.L. Mencken once described the clergy as ticket speculators outside the gates of heaven. It is not uncommon even now for skeptics and others to be anticlerical. There are always many justifying examples. In general, however, the modern, well-trained, and well-disciplined ministers, priests, or rabbis hold places of public respect equal to those of scientists, educators, poets, and the like. They are regarded as makers and transmitters of culture, and as useful, responsible community figures who, more often than not, succeed in practicing what they preach.

Rather than being satirized, ministers often are objects of intense solicitude. There are frequent articles, reports, and studies about the plight of harassed, overworked, and underpaid clergy. Under headlines like "Why Ministers Are Breaking Down," they will list, anonymously, "brilliant" clerics who have been drained, exhausted, and washed up at what would otherwise be the height of their powers. Then follows an analysis of the minister's job—like an equestrian who is ordered to ride off in all directions at the same time. The blame often is placed squarely on congregations for failing to understand and appreciate the impossible demands made on their spiritual leaders.

My own feeling, developed over the years, is that the "driven" clergy are frequently the drivers. That is, they drive themselves for inner reasons they do not understand. The fact that many ministers do eventually end up in intensive therapy is not an offense attributable solely to voracious congregations. In fact, it is not an offense at all. Few congregations are exempt from the need for regular self-study and process review, preferably with skilled help. But in the selection and training of clergy early therapeutic "vaccination" and regular "booster shots" can fend off a lot of heartaches and breakdowns. We understand very easily the necessity of ministers' warmth toward others, but we are slower to realize the importance for clergy to like and respect themselves enough to cherish, conserve, and pace themselves.

Ministers can get themselves into all kinds of trouble. Few congregants really know how often ministers work thirteen or fourteen hours a day, seven days a week, months at a time, if that is what they choose to do. I say *choose* though the choice may not necessarily be conscious. But the fact remains that ministers may, if they know enough about themselves, choose to live relatively normal and balanced lives of work and play, study and recreation, activity and rest. In brief, ministers can learn to say no as well as yes. And I do not merely mean no to others. I mean no to themselves too. One of the most important yeses ministers should learn to say to themselves is, Yes, I also am a person of flesh and not of stardust.

There are few professions in which there is not more work than a person can ever hope to get done. The ministry shares this plight, but the minister's task in coping with it is not essentially different from that in other responsible and burdened occupations.

Those who go into the ministry should expect to work hard and still live with the frustrations of never getting their work completed. The ability to pace themselves, conserve their energies, and diversify their interests and enjoyments is not something congregations can do for ministers. Congregations can do this with them, by making sensible and reasonable administrative arrangements and by fully assuming lay responsibilities, but first ministers must have the inner security to enable congregations to do that, and the will to get off their own backs. They must love and respect themselves and their congregants enough to want *all* in the community to be whole.

Mr. Justice Brennan of the United States Supreme Court received a letter that read in part: "Would you use your influence to help my boy to become a Judge. He don't like hard work and I figure that sitting on a bench would suit him just fine."

No man or woman who "don't like hard work" will find the ministry a congenial place. On the other hand, for those who are unable to learn to cherish themselves enough to live broadly and variously, with due respect for their own limitations and needs, the ministry is a poor place.

It is characteristic of congregations to want professional leaders to whom the religious life is an all-pervasive, full-time, and exacting calling that makes extraordinary claims on intelligence, sensitivity, and conscience. Ministers, in other words, are embodiments of spiritual specialization. This is not to say that laypersons desire ministers to be ethereal and otherworldly. The evidence from surveys done among Unitarian Universalist congregations indicates unmistakably that while preferred ministers are scholarly, idealistic, and responsive, they are also, by overwhelming choice, earthy and pragmatic.

The key attributes seem to be intensity and specialization. Laypersons sense that their religion is of necessity relatively cloistered. Preoccupations and distractions limit the scope of spiritual interest and cultivation. At first this sounds like a reversal of terms. After all, it is generally assumed that if anyone lives in a cloister, it is the clergy. But it depends on the kind of cloister we are talking about. If daily life, with its numerous demands and responses, is viewed as a cloister, then it is the layperson's life that is isolated from intimation and insights of spirit.

My years of association with laypersons, of enjoying the privilege of knowing them intimately, persuade me that this is a truth experienced deeply enough to be the basic motive of congregations in wanting ministers in their midst. Here are those whose only reason for being, as far as their professional lives are concerned, is to bring moral idealism to every realm of human experience. Here is a person who, by the deliberate deed of a congregation, is given the time, freedom, and sustenance to study, speak, and act on the ethical and spiritual issues of living and to help make more intelligible, to those who cannot claim such time and freedom, the religious resources available to them.

When congregations or parishioners experience disappointment, it is traceable mainly to a shattering of the image just described. If ministers fail, even unwittingly, to be the embodiments of the full-time religious life; if they fail, in some instance, to look at all aspects of life—personal, political, workaday, social—with religious insight and commitment, they are disappointments to those who accept their ministry.

I shudder as I write these words, because they mean that ministers are destined to fail in their chosen vocation. No matter how competent they become, they can never achieve enough. This makes of the ministry a very wide place and a very long road.

If the ministry is a call, it is a call not away from humanity but into it, deeply into it. It is not a summons to detachment, to become a Captain McWhirr, whom Joseph Conrad described in *Typhoon* as sailing "over the surface of the oceans as some . . . go skimming through years of existence to sink gently into a placid grave, ignorant of life to the last, without ever having been made to see all it may contain of perfidy, of violence and of error."

It is the most human thing in the world to flee from the slings and arrows of the mortal condition, and the ministry can be easily taken as a flight from being fully human—a kind of semidivine posture of being above the common embarrassment, doubt, and shame. But the only meaningful sense of the word *ministry* is one that speaks of a human fellowship of joy and pain and believes that persons do not come to themselves and to one another until they share the deepest levels of caring and compassion.

To minister—and here the word embraces laity and clergy alike—is to be called out of our pretensions, poses, and protective façades and into the great, open, windy world, where we are at least alive, even if tremblingly so, and where the chances of confirming the sanctities of our blundering hearts are endless.

To be a minister does not mean to be religious in a particular way, to cultivate certain techniques, which any bright woman or man can master, but to be a person. It is not some ecclesiastical act that makes a minister, but participation in the lives of humans, individual and associated, though it often brings one into painful relations.

The tremendous thing that is involved here is not a simple question of personal virtue or professional rectitude, but a genuine affirmation of the world: to love and live in the world for the

world's own sake. And I am not talking about phony attempts to
feint people into a position where the minister can get past their
guard and whisper moral blandishments.

If we truly love the world, so that we can dare to defy it, we
will have to get much closer to it than any phony worldliness permits. We will have to immerse ourselves in its sorrows, taste its bitter cups, and open our hearts to its most painful conflicts and
tensions. Then and only then can our lives speak truth to the
world in the spirit of love. In the more traditional religious ranks
there is a caustic observation about clergy who stroke the cross but
are very careful never to get crucified. Liberal ministers have their
own unmoral equivalent in absent-minded wandering from room
to room in humanity's tragic house, making gestures toward sisterhood and brotherhood, mumbling something about all-powerful
reason, and contributing their own share of shallow faith with
which religion so often pollutes the human atmosphere. In more
ways than we like to contemplate, we disgrace with our actions the
burning life-giving zeal we preach with our lips. Theodore Parker
said: "I determined to preach nothing as religion which I had not
experienced inwardly, and made my own, knowing it by heart."

What is it, then, that constitutes *ministry*? And I put it this way
purposely to include the work of the laity as well as the clergy.
Louis Lavelle describes it in his *Meaning of Holiness* when he
speaks of those men and women who through their presence succeed in evoking in others an "interior quality."

The worst this world can visit on human spirit and flesh is the
emptying of life, the sickening sense of nothingness. And in a
world throbbing with technology and technique, with hard sell,
hard play, and furious events, people spin until there is no inner
life left in them. They become clothes without bodies and bodies
without souls; they become not persons but masks, routines, objects, and roles: images without substance. Ministry is the restora-
tion of an interior quality to life, a substance and a sustenance to
the human interior. Ministry is the rehabilitation of people inwardly, an engagement in the kinds of relationships and advoca-

cies that make persons of people, that imagine, anticipate, and empower the soul.

Wallace Stevens has a poem called "The Man with the Blue Guitar." It echoes Picasso's painting.

The man bent over his guitar,
A shearsman of sorts. The day was green.

They said, "You have a blue guitar,
You do not play things as they are."

The man replied, "Things as they are
Are changed upon the blue guitar."

And they said then, "But play you must,
A tune beyond us, yet ourselves,

A tune upon the blue guitar
Of things exactly as they are."

A ministry is a blue guitar—something deeply embedded in the mystery of what we are as human beings. There can be no escape from doing something with things as they are, exactly as they are.

But one thing ministers cannot do. They cannot leave things as they are. They must play a tune beyond. Things must be changed on the blue guitar.

It is generally assumed that churches go looking for people. I went looking for a church—the right church for me. A conscious-ness of the possibilities in the Unitarian movement grew on me slowly. The merging of Unitarianism and Universalism was then only a dream. My Quaker acquaintances, who were aware of my unresolved dilemma, made gentle suggestions. As with so many I have met since, the unique qualities of Unitarian and Universalist churches were unknown to me. My first tentative visits were in-teresting but uninspiring. The intellectual caliber of the preaching was cuts above what I had known, but I happened to go to where the congregations were sparse, the ambience somewhat stiff, and the forms of worship too traditionally Protestant for my taste. But

I took to reading whatever I could lay my hands on about the legacy of the liberal spirit in religion, which kept my curiosity alive. Then one Sunday in 1941 I found myself listening to John Haynes Holmes at New York's Community Church, an institution with a long Unitarian heritage. The congregation was then meeting in Town Hall, hardly an exalted setting, but Holmes created a temple of the human spirit just with his presence and preaching. The congregation was vibrant and an eloquent symbol of human diversity. The service was religious, deeply religious, yet there were no divisive, mind-splitting doctrinal elements.

During that hour I knew that if the Unitarian ministry was exciting enough to produce the fervent witness of a John Haynes Holmes, it might just possibly do the same for me. A door was open, and I wasted no time going through it. By the following summer I was enrolled in the Harvard Divinity School, with the warm encouragement and backing of the American Unitarian Association and its then-president Frederick May Eliot.

I had reservations then, just as I have now. I don't think that a religious liberal should ever be without them. As my first year of theological education began, I was asked by Stephen Fritchman, editor of the *Christian Register*, the official Unitarian magazine, to write an article on why I was entering the Unitarian ministry. In it I expressed my resentment at the bias that so obviously discouraged women from joining our ministry. My hope that this would end has, in recent years, been exultantly realized. Also, then, as now, I was distressed by the overwhelming number of white and middle-class people in our movement. Our denominational record of the number of blacks in the pulpit or the pew continues to be a sorry one indeed. My commitment to changing that record is strong, in faithfulness to the opportunities to unfold, which the Unitarian Universalist ministry has brought me. I am continually amazed and inspired by the growth of what Emerson called "faith, admiration and sympathy," which I find afforded by my calling, and especially by the congregations it has been my privilege to serve. Each has given memorable lessons of freedom in community.

Getting from Sunday to Monday

A person has no religion who has not slowly and painfully gathered one together, adding to it, shaping it; and one's religion is never complete and final, it seems, but must always be undergoing modification.

D.H. LAWRENCE

There are very different notions of what precisely a religion is. Consider, for example, the covenant of All Souls Unitarian Universalist Church in Indianapolis. I served as minister there from 1954 to 1959, and during those years we planned, financed, and built an entirely new church plant. I remember having long conversations with the architects, especially about how to express spatially the congregation's covenant: "Love is the spirit of this church and service is its law; to dwell together in peace, to seek the truth in love, and to help one another: This is our covenant." The architects sensitively probed with us why there were no theological doctrines set forth in this statement. It simply formulates a human purpose on which we are all united, we explained, and allows the widest possible latitude of individual theological belief. One of the architects asked whether a Baptist, Presbyterian, or Catholic could join our church. Of course, we answered, though practically speaking they might not want to because our statement leaves out matters that they might strongly want to include. But there are no barriers as far as we are concerned to anyone who wants to join us in furthering the purposes set forth in our covenant. This applies to Jews, Buddhists, Muslims, atheists, and agnostics, as well as to Christians.

Many years ago William Channing Gannett formulated the basic operational principles of our liberal religious movement in a brief statement that is as fresh as if it had just been written. He said: "*Freedom* is our method in religion; *reason* is our guide in religion; *fellowship* is our spirit in religion; *character* is our test in religion; *service* is our aim in religion." Once again, there is nothing about theological doctrine here; the concern is with a spirit, a method, a purpose.

We are forever being asked: But what, then, makes you a *church*? To those who ask, *church* obviously means required assent to certain concrete doctrinal beliefs. Not so among Unitarian Universalists. Whether the subject is God, Jesus, or immortality, there are widely varying convictions and questions among us, beneath which there is a unifying affirmation: the right of persons to make their own theological decisions. The prevailing notion of a church is that it conforms to a conventional pattern, which includes a creed, submission to authority (of holy writ, institution, hierarchy, and so on), and participation in prescribed rites and sacraments. To the uninitiated, the most puzzling feature of the Unitarian Universalist religion is its disregard of these ecclesiastical conventions. When they hear of this open process for the first time, some are confused. Others, coming suddenly upon it, fairly glow. "I've been a Unitarian Universalist for years without knowing it" is a familiar refrain. Many do not really know what to do with religiousness when it expresses itself outside the enclosures that convention has carefully labeled religion. For those not so inhibited in their spiritual pilgrimage, here, as a beginning, are some questions to try, to see if they have an intimate ring:

> I simply cannot accept religious beliefs on trust alone. Is there a church for me?

I believe in many things: a deep religious chord within my being, essential human dignity, the efficacy of human effort, the search for larger truths, hunger for a caring community, the compelling need for ethical disciplines, the necessities of practiced human sisterhood and brotherhood, but I cannot bind my beliefs to a creedal test, nor place them beyond rational criticism. What church would welcome me?

In the end churches always seem to insist that the essence of their truth is revealed and complete. Does any church embrace the idea that even the essence of truth is an emerging, not a finished, thing?

Why shouldn't children be encouraged to discover religion in their own unfolding lives rather than have it drilled into them by indoctrination, no matter how well meaning? What church practices this?

Can any church be effective as a cohesive community and still urge its members to be their free, responsible, individual selves?

There is self-evident beauty and inspiration in all of the world's religious faiths. Is there a church that welcomes and reverences the insights of all significant spiritual systems?

Can persons from many religious backgrounds—Christian, Jewish, Buddhist, Muslim—find a church where all are welcome without conversion or renunciation?

I want to be free to wonder about—even doubt—the existence of God, the nature of God, the effectiveness of prayer, the value of the Bible, the possibility of immortality, and still be religious. Where is the church that does not label honest doubt "heresy" and where "heretics" are welcome?

If you find a gleam of recognition in these questions, if they reflect some of your own thoughts, experiences, and searching, there is probably an exciting place for you in the Unitarian Universalist fold.

For us, the vital task in religion is to get from Sunday to Monday: to carry our serious concern with spirituality and religious living from the protected atmosphere of a worship service into the flesh and blood realities of daily living. Religions generally emphasize salvation, and most religions speak of salvation in terms of creeds, ceremonies, sacraments, and catechisms. We speak warmly of salvation also, but in terms of character. We choose to think of it as dependent on deeds, not creeds. We also think of it as pertaining to the herein, not just the hereafter.

"What must I do to be saved?" That was the question the jailer asked the apostle Paul. His answer, as recorded in the Book of Acts, was crucial. One might say it marked a point of no return for orthodox Christianity. Recall this biblical incident: In the city of Philippi, in the Roman colony of Macedonia, Paul and his associate, Silas, were brought before the local magistrate for preaching religious doctrines frowned upon by the empire. After some manhandling by a mob, they were unceremoniously thrown into a prison cell where they immediately began praying and singing hymns. In the midst of this informal service, a violent earthquake shook the cell door open and split the prisoners' chains. The jailer, a sound sleeper who had evidently dozed through both the singing and the earthquake, thus proving himself to be a person of tolerably quiet conscience, awoke to find the prison doors open. Panic-stricken that he had permitted his prisoners to escape, he drew his sword to commit suicide. In the nick of time, Paul cried out: "Do not harm yourself. We are here." Overcome with gratitude, the jailer rushed toward Paul and Silas, pleading: "What must I do to be saved? And Paul replied: "Believe in the Lord Jesus, and you will be saved, you and your household."

I want to be fair to Paul, whose hymn to love and "When I was a child . . . ," both in I Corinthians, are among the most sublime of religious writings. What we have is a story *about* Paul, not *by* Paul. But be that as it may, whenever I read this story I think of all the answers Paul might have given. He might even have asked some questions of his own: "What do you mean *saved*? Do you mean how can you live a juster, kinder, more faithful life, or do you mean how can you get to heaven?"

Paul simply assumed, according to the story, as so many clergy have gone assuming ever since, that the jailer was only interested in getting his endangered soul into celestial safekeeping. He further assumed that no desire could be dearer to the jailer's heart than to escape this wicked world. No consideration was apparently given to the possibility that life is an exceedingly precious gift, that it is a great privilege to be alive and to have opportunities to do better with a life than one has done. Nothing of that. Paul, we are told, simply blurted out a formula. And not merely a formula, but, from his point of view, *the* formula: "Believe in the Lord Jesus, and you will be saved, you and your household."

Here was the track of authoritarianism on which orthodox Christianity would run from the days of the Book of Acts to our own. Did it occur to Paul that the jailer might have some thoughts and insights of his own worth probing and nurturing? There is nothing of this in the story. Paul, it would seem, saw no reason to encourage the jailer to reflect on his traumatic experience, to ponder in his heart and conscience what might be found there. No words are attributed to Paul that might have moved Christianity in the direction of freedom and deepened accountability. Instead, a dogma is uttered, saying, in effect, this is not something to examine, to weigh, to test by experience. No, this is something you simply accept.

Unitarian Universalists don't buy it. The kind of religion that commands our allegiance is the kind that respects our ability to make considered religious decisions. In this sense, we feel much more at home with certain biblical portrayals of Jesus than with this depiction of Paul. The jailer asked a heartfelt question. He had been through a shattering experience. It made him think of ultimate things: "What must I do to be saved?" What a glorious opportunity for Paul to tell of Jesus's approach to the art of living. But there is not one word of the teachings of Jesus. All that is offered is a theological doctrine; nothing about love, nothing about an aspiring morality, nothing about bold goodwill.

Compare this with a similar recorded experience in the life of Jesus. A wealthy and deeply troubled young man came to Jesus with a question. "Rabbi," he asked, in more cultivated tones than the jailer's, "what must I do to inherit eternal life?" Jesus did not answer, "Believe in me and you will walk heaven's golden streets." Instead, we are told, Jesus encouraged the young man to guide his life by the great ethical teachings of the prophets. Forget about your wealth and bring riches to the lives of others!

The young man went away crestfallen, for he had great possessions. He wanted a formula. He would have liked talking with Paul much better. Perhaps this is why traditional Christianity became a religion *about* Jesus rather than a religion *of* Jesus. Yet, who knows what transformation might have occurred in the young man when, in the privacy of his thoughts, he began to reflect on the moral challenge the strange rabbi had given him.

For us, salvation is not an otherworldly journey, flown on wings of dogma. It is ethical striving and moral growth: respect for the personalities and experiences of others; faith in human dignity and potentiality; aversion to sanctimony and bigotry; reverence for the gift of life; confidence in a true harmony of mind and spirit, of nature and human nature; faith in the ability to give and receive love; and a quest for broad, encompassing religious expression—spiritual yet practical, personal and communal.

This is what we mean when we say we believe in salvation by character. Perhaps it would be more accurate to say that we believe salvation *is* character, for we do not mean that character saves us from the flames of hell or takes us to the bliss of heaven. We do not profess to know, as a community of faith, the precise dimensions of immortality. But we are sure of this: The inner life, shaped by the power of high and sane ideals, brings to human souls the finest, most enduring satisfactions and makes of our humanity a source of strength, even in utmost tribulation. This is what we mean by salvation, and what serves so well in life could not possibly serve less well in afterlife.

We believe that our humanness is punished *by* our sins, not *for* them, and that the evil we do lives with us. By the same token, we believe that we are enriched by our virtues, and that the good we do lives with us and beyond us as a benediction of peace in our own lives and in the life of humanity.

We believe that corporate religion—the church—has no higher object than helping us to get from Sunday to Monday, taking our Sunday processions into our Monday behavior; in short, when we talk of salvation, we talk of making religion a sustained and sustaining force in our daily lives, We do not say that religion has nothing to do with the afterlife, but we do say that it has everything to do with this life.

What Do You Say After You Say "I'm a Unitarian Universalist"?

> Actually, we have to make the best judgments we can about what is right, and then we have to bet on it by trying to make ourselves act on it, without being sure about it.
>
> ARNOLD TOYNBEE

In his delightful volume, *Born Again Unitarian Universalism*, F. Forrester Church, minister of All Souls Unitarian Church in New York City, recounts a conversation at a stiff dinner party. Seated between strangers and caught off guard, he let the cat slip out.

"You are a what?"

"A Unitarian Universalist."

"Oh, I see," he says, but obviously he doesn't. He is rescued by the woman to our right.

"I've never really understood just what it is you Unitarians believe. You *are* Christians, aren't you?"

"Not exactly. I mean, we were and some of us still are but most of us are not."

"You don't believe in Jesus?"

"Not in an orthodox way, certainly. Many of us value his teachings but few, if any of us, believe that he was resurrected on the third day or that he was God."

"What about immortality?"

"Well, I guess you'd have to say that we're pretty much divided on that one."

"But at least you all believe in God?" interrupts the man across the table. . . .

"Not exactly. Many of us do, if each in his or her own way. Others of us do not find the concept of God a useful one."

"What then *do* you believe?" our bewildered hostess politely asks.

A conversation of this kind is instantly recognized and appreciated by most Unitarian Universalists, with an "Ay, there's the rub." There is an initial difficulty that confronts us when we are asked point blank what we believe. Those who ask usually expect a creedal answer: "I (we) believe in God, the Father Almighty, etc." But we cannot give that kind of answer because we are a creedless church. There are two very compelling (to us) reasons for this. First, we are persuaded that it is spiritually depriving to state the intellectual content of religious belief in fixed and final form; we are convinced that humans are created to be capable of growth in their understandings of truth. So we have decided that a formal creed is a hindrance rather than a help in religion, and we have eliminated it from our church, choosing instead to set forth statements of purpose and principle, which by a democratic process of study and discussion we can refine as we see fit. Second, we are bound together by ties that we find deeper and more satisfying than those of creedal affirmation; we are bound together by a spirit of enriching our individual lives within a framework of caring community and of improving the social order. Within this unity of spirit we discover that it is invigorating to hold a wide variety of theological beliefs; we have no need of uniformity of belief among our members.

By its very nature, a creed is final and binding upon all who profess it. It is held to be outside the reach of questioning examination. Its origin in divine inspiration is assumed. Actually, if the historic church creeds were divinely revealed, they came into being in a strikingly human manner. There were more than two centuries of speculation, debate, and bitter strife before the first "final" Christian creed, the Nicene, became compulsory, on pain of excommunication, even death. It and its companion piece, the Apostles' Creed, cannot be viewed historically as anything but a string of compromises, based on an accommodation of contending views.

The traditional creeds are human creations, and they were probably the best attainable expressions of Christian belief in the third and fourth centuries. What we cannot accept is that these creeds should be binding on this and future generations. To us, the creation of a religious way of life is far too important to be left to the distant past's propounders of doctrine. We are Unitarian Universalists, not by substituting one confession of faith for another, but by opening our minds to receive truth and inspiration from every possible source—even from the ancient creeds, if by critical examination they throw genuine light on current concerns.

The most fundamental of all Unitarian Universalist principles, then, is personal freedom of religious belief—the principle of the free mind. But freedom, as Henry Whitney Bellows taught his congregation more than a century ago, "has no power to produce anything. It merely leaves the faculties free to act." Freedom is not aimless wandering with no duties attached. The freedom we hold so dear is the freedom of our faculties to act in behalf of what challenges and transforms our lives, our passage from birth to death. For us, this freedom to grow, to act, and to redeem is not based on external authority. It is established in our inward parts. No priest or pastor dictates. No Holy Writ dictates. No creed dictates what must be believed.

For those who are frankly appalled at the "burden" of such liberal spiritual freedom, the attractions of external authority are understandably great. I was once reproached by an acquaintance of impressive intellectual gifts and scientific achievements for doing a profound disservice by exhorting people to try to work out their own religious answers. "Religion," he said, "is a specialty that should be left to experts."

Unitarian Universalists are people who cannot leave their religious beliefs in the care of "experts." For us, the most vital faith about the human possibility is this: We must be free to grow in spirit. There is no area of life in which it is more important for us to be free than in the realm of spirit.

Those who honestly differ with us (and we respect them for it) argue that human nature requires authoritative religious guidance, or our inherent proneness to sin will corrupt and destroy. Yet when we begin to examine closely the "authoritative" religious guidance, what do we discover? The church that boasts authority to dictate beliefs is, whatever its claims, a human institution, and its "final truths" are only conclusions of previous leaders. The same is true of the Bible. It was written by mortals. No creed exists that was not originally hammered out, under pressure, by human beings like ourselves.

Churches, Bibles, and creeds are the creations of humans who once exercised their freedom to create. Is there any reason we should expect to do less? We accept the birth of a new age in all kinds of human undertakings; why not in religion as well? Human beings are still in the learning stage about everything from evolution to communication. All over the lot, concepts of truth and reality are in flux. The traditions and habits on which the religions of past millennia were founded have elements that are enduring and elements that are not. Either we go forward with religious sentiments and formulations appropriate for our time, or time will leave some radioactive remnant of us cringing in ancient spiritual caves.

The distinctive characteristic of religious liberals is their insistence that they will not lock their present and future in religion into the tutelage of the past. They will attempt to learn all that the past can teach, but they will do their own thinking about current matters of faith and belief.

Believing that spirituality is the power of understanding life, we Unitarian Universalists affirm within the community of the church our dependence on our thinking to generate significance and vitality. In Forrester Church's words (in *Born Again Unitarian Universalism*):

> We value one another's thinking. We respect one another's
> search. We honor it even when it differs from our own. We

resist imposing our perception of truth upon one another. Embracing a kind of theological pluralism, we affirm the human importance of our joint quest for meaning in life without insisting upon the ultimacy of any single set of theological criteria. . . . At our best, we move . . . to a fundamental trust in our own and one another's inherent ability to make life meaningful.

In a Unitarian Universalist congregation, an agnostic may sit beside one who believes in a personal God; at the after-service coffee hour a believer in reincarnation may stand chatting with one who affirms "utter extinction." Such are our diversities in theological belief.

We are together in our devotion to spiritual freedom; each challenged to live by a considered, examined, experienced covenant with self, others, and life as a whole; each understanding, even hoping, that beliefs may change as insights deepen and life teaches.

Earthy and Practical Reason

Since ours is such a free and creedless church, are we, as some claim, nothing but "a haven for people who can't quite make up their minds"? In *The Unitarian Universalist Pocket Guide*, David Rankin illustrates this charge:

> One wit has written that a Unitarian Universalist is a person who walks a thin line between confusion and indecision.
>
> Another wit has written that if you are a Unitarian Universalist, bigots burn a question mark on your lawn.
>
> So much for wits!

Yes, we have our anxious moments about the freedom we cherish. But second only to the free mind is our belief in reason and responsibility. Freedom requires responsibility, and responsibility requires reason. Humans must accept responsibility for their choices and for their acts. We believe that this sense of responsibility reflects the teachings of the great biblical prophets, from

Amos to Jesus. We believe that our religious concept of moral and ethical responsibility is much more in tune with reality, and much more productive than the traditional doctrine of human nature's inherent depravity through "original sin."

"Why am I such a failure?" said the woman sitting in my study. She looked like anything but a failure. She and her husband and children were my good friends. I had been in their home many times and was impressed with the apparent affection and openness of family ties. Both parents worked. There were no unusual financial problems. Yet this woman was struggling with an insidious sense of guilt and inadequacy. A "tradition of inferiority" was poisoning her life.

Where does this tradition come from? For women, the punishing effects of this tradition are amplified by the deep strains of sexism embedded in our culture. But why are men, as well as women, so conscious of their failings and limitations that they are unable to think of good things as flowing from their lives? One of the most widespread causes, in my opinion, is the doctrine of original sin, stressed in early religious training and magnified until it comes to be regarded, deep in the recesses of personality, as an innate evil from which there is no real escape.

Please don't misunderstand me. I believe in sin. Looking within me and around me, how could I, or anyone, believe otherwise? But nothing is more appalling to me than the crippling effects of religions that fill persons with a sense of their hopeless condition, their wicked and disgraceful alienation from goodness and virtue. Each person experiences enough emotional conflict, enough harm done others, enough regret, enough self-reproach to give force to the doctrines of original sin and total depravity. The eloquent, remorseful outcry of the apostle Paul vividly expresses the traumatic clash between aspiration and action:

> For the good that I would, I do not: but the evil which I would not, that I do. O wretched man that I am! Who shall deliver me from the body of this death? (Romans 1).

With such a ghastly assessment of human nature, sharply contrasted with the perfection and beauty of God, how could one avoid the conclusion that the sources of the good life are nowhere to be found within the human frame? But a realistic study of human nature reveals a plethora of impulses and a rich diversity of motives within which the process of moral selection proceeds. We find some things are better and others worse, by trial and error, by measurements of happiness and welfare, by comparison and reflection. This is how we humans cultivate responsible behavior. For Unitarian Universalists, a chief resource is reason. With us reason holds a place ordinarily accorded to revelation in other religions. Those who are likely to behave best exercise their reason most.

Thus I, for one, remain hopeful about the human estate. I find a basic capacity for goodness in the human animal—a goodness that is not meaningfully negated by the "fall."

This does not mean that I am unmindful of the limitations of human reason, nor that I look upon it as an infallible guide. In the Unitarian Universalist way of life there are no infallible guides. But central to my faith and that of my liberal religious forebears is the notion that reason is crucial to our functioning. How else shall we discuss our feelings of truth, beauty, and goodness? These matters do not, as some would say, defy discussion. Our religious community, our church, is grounded in just such communication. E. Burdette Backus, one of my early mentors in the ministry, used to describe our reasoning ability as an instrument that developed in the process of evolution, enabling us to satisfy our needs more adequately. In one sermon he wrote:

> It had originally a very earthy and practical purpose, namely that of solving the problems that press in upon . . . daily life. Although it continues this immediately pressing function, it has far outsoared it and seeks to penetrate beyond the stars to find an answer to the riddle of the universe. Our reason makes many mistakes; it is frequently taken captive by our desires, so that we believe things not because they are

true but because we want to believe them. It cannot give us absolute and final certainty, but it has established a substantial body of verified truth; it is steadily increasing the amount of that truth. For all its limitations it serves us very well, and those who advocate its abandonment are simply telling us as we grope our way through the dark by the light of a candle to blow out the light.

Of course there are irrational elements in our experience of ourselves and, seemingly, of our cosmos. But to comprehend them, to understand them, perhaps even to transcend them—how else but by reason?

Unitarian Universalism, then, is a community of faith, with individual freedom as its method and with reason as its guide. It should not be assumed, however, that we practice reason in an austere and overly solemn manner. When we succeed in seizing upon the finer and more elevating aspects of experience, projecting them enlarged and colorfully enhanced upon the canvases of life, they become the source of the warmest joy and blessedness. Our purpose is to enable heart and mind to capture realizations of what life can be when humans live up to their best. Through expanded imagination, awakened conscience, and enriched beauty there springs into being a spiritual fellowship whose inspiration to deepen satisfaction and more ample living has magnificent force.

Susan B. Anthony, the famous champion of woman suffrage in the early days of that movement, and a Unitarian, celebrated our position on reason with a telling phrase: "Truth for authority, not authority for truth." That's it! Discover what commends itself to your reason as truth and then accept that as your authority. And by working at it faithfully, with one another's help, we can become better, wiser, and more loving human beings. We might even help this to become a better, wiser, and more loving world.

The path of the liberal religious journey leads from freedom, through reason, to a third fundamental principle: a generous, appreciative acceptance of differing views and practices.

Unity with Diversity

Churches are voluntary social institutions, sometimes warmly sociable, sometimes less so. Voluntary social institutions have an intriguing double function. They are at once the cause and the effect of the interests they represent. Nurturant families are the outgrowth of mutual love, and they are the producers of nurturing personalities. Admirable schools are products of concern for the learning process, and they inspire love of learning in those who participate in them. Churches are created by religious interest and enthusiasm, and participation in the activities of church life awaken and deepen spiritual aspirations.

If only the first part of this equation is emphasized, it encourages some to proclaim that churches are not necessary to the religious life ("I can get all the religion I need working in my garden"). When only the second part is stressed, it tempts some to conclude that churches are the sole source of spirituality. Each view is fragmentary and one-sided. All voluntary institutions are at once the yield and source of the convictions, carings, and concerns they embody. Concern for the environment draws people together into environmental and conservation associations, and these associations in turn stimulate higher levels of social policy and personal consciousness. Love of the spiritual life draws religionists together; organized religion encourages the further quest for spiritual affections and understandings.

Most churches find their bond in scriptural or creedal affirmations. Membership is based on a more or less uniform profession of theological belief, usually accompanied by a rite or rites.

We Unitarian Universalists fashion our bond differently. It is our faith and practice that people can covenant to work together for the deepening of spiritual life, the strengthening of moral character, and the improvement of society without conforming to a set pattern of theological doctrines. In fact, we go well beyond this to declare our conviction that differing theological views are natural and healthy and that attempts to enforce conformity are deadening and potentially destructive. History is witness to the horrors of religious intolerance.

We hold that churches are voluntary communities striving for togetherness in difference, for fellowship combined with individual freedom, for the right to be oneself joined with vital participation in society. The goal of organized Unitarian Universalism is to provide maximum freedom combined with full fellowship for each individual. Truth, we recognize, is vast and many-sided. Why should we all have the same theology? It is a basic part of our faith that people of widely differing religious backgrounds and meaningful symbol systems can work cheerfully and productively together under the same denominational roof, strengthening and challenging one another, for the great common tasks of making human life more splendid, more precious, and more secure. This stance is an eminently practical one of measuring religion by the fruit it bears rather than the bark it wears. By making this concept explicit in the organized life of the church, we unfurl standards of value found within experience itself and make them subject to the judgment and conscience of the people who actually constitute the community of the institution.

Serious seekers of what Unitarian Universalists *really* believe must first be encouraged to set aside their predilection for the theological definitions that describe most churches. They must also be urged to suspend the notion that there are only two alternatives: accepting a creedal religion or rejecting church life altogether. Ours is very definitely a different kind of church, which requires a different kind of definition. Yet, let there be no mistake about the fact that the Unitarian Universalist fellowship is a purposeful, positive, organized religious movement, dedicated to the spiritual, moral, and social fulfillment of the gift of life. Let those who believe that they must surrender their intellectual freedom in order to enter a community of faith take notice.

Our churches reach out to all who catch a vision of filling the empty places in their lives by placing principles of freedom, responsibility, reason, and tolerance above uniform theological doctrines. Our churches are free associations of those who fashion their own personal theologies, unconstrained by institutional dogmas or ecclesiastical authorities. Our covenant is to strive together by every honest means to discover and nurture the highest forms of life that creative experience can devise. Religion for us is no insulated segment of life. It is our entire being in search of meaning.

We are respectful of the history out of which we have come and through which we have endured for more than four hundred years. But we are bound by no historic model. We continue to evolve by the light of our growing understanding of ourselves and our world. We feel obliged by the very urgency of religion to seek and experiment with more effective forms of teaching our members, young and old, with more compelling and inspiring arts of worship, with more energetic and adequate methods of public witness, and with more moving and sustaining sources of comfort and courage in the high adventure of living our lives in examined, loving, and transforming ways.

How Did We Get This Way?

Heir of all the ages, I,
Heir of all that they have wrought,
Struggle stern, adventure high,
All their wealth of precious thought.

JULIA CAROLINE RIPLEY DORR

The plane on which I traveled landed at the Athens airport in the eerie half-light of dawn. By the time customs formalities were over, the rising sun had placed a halo on the nearby hills. A taxi sped me along the Pireus and headed up a broad avenue toward the city's heart. Suddenly, there it was: the Acropolis, silhouetted against a brilliant morning sky! Transported through time as well as space, I had arrived at one of the cradles of my liberal faith. It wasn't Unitarian Universalism Socrates had in mind, but he was seeding the soil when he said to Crito:

> Do not mind whether the teachers of philosophy are good or bad, but think only of Philosophy herself. Try to examine her well and truly; and if she be evil, seek to turn all away from her; but if she be what I believe she is, then follow her and serve her, and be of good cheer.

With such words were laid the foundations of the free human spirit, the examined life, and the endless quest for elusive, redemptive truth. Ancient Athens was one of the planting places of liberal religion. Take the word *heretic* and forget for the moment how it has been loaded with negative baggage. *Heretic* is a Greek word that means "able to choose." Think of that. Heretics are persons of independent mind who, as Socrates taught, do not simply accept beliefs because they happen to be dominant in the society or because they are taught by their churches, but they accept them on the basis of their own testing, their own independent thought. They consider different possibilities and are able to choose.

On another journey, it was my good fortune to spend an hour in Israel with the great Jewish philosopher and theologian Martin Buber. He was a gnome-like man, barely five feet tall, with a huge head and a magnificent, flowing white beard. His eyes were large, brown, and compassionate. His study, in a shaded, one-story, stuccoed house in Jerusalem, deserved a Dickens to describe: Victorian desk and divan, a lamp that must have been designed soon after the invention of the electric light bulb, random heaps of books, brochures, pamphlets, periodicals, and manuscripts.

As he began to talk, I scribbled furiously. Suddenly there was silence, and when I looked up, Buber was smiling. "Mr. Mendelsohn," he said, "either you can take notes without really listening, or you can really listen without taking notes." It was said with no trace of harshness. Firmly, I closed my notebook and "really listened." He said: "Throughout the world, there is a spiritual front on which a secret, silent struggle is being waged between the desire to be on life's side and the desire to destroy. This is the most important front of all—more important than any military, political, or economic front. It is the front on which *souls are moulded.*"

My question was the obvious one: "What can individuals do to tip the balance?"

Buber gazed out the window for a moment; then he turned to me and said:

No one can chart a day-to-day course for anyone else. Life can only be determined by each situation as it arises. We all have our chances. From the time we rise in the morning until the time we retire at night we have meetings with others. Sometimes we even meet ourselves! We see our families at breakfast. We go to work with others. We meet people in the streets. We attend gatherings with others. Always there are others. What we do with each of these meetings is what counts. The future is more determined by this than by ideologies and proclamations.

In sitting with Buber I felt that I was in the presence of another remarkable Hebrew prophet—one whose lineage extended directly to Amos, Hosea, Isaiah, Jeremiah, and Jesus. I was moved, as in Athens, by a sense of discovery of the roots of my Unitarian Universalist religion.

Modern liberal religion gratefully acknowledges its debt to these two founts of reverence for human dignity and ethical imperatives: ancient Athens and ancient Israel. And I, for one, acknowledge also that just as Socrates was not much heeded in ancient Athens, neither was Buber, an advocate of Jewish-Arab reconciliation, much heeded in modern Israel.

The Christian origins of our movement are anchored in a long, shared history of reverence for the moral example and teachings of Jesus, as exemplified in the Beatitudes and the Sermon on the Mount. We realize that there are many complications in making a historical assessment of Jesus. Most of us hold that, on the basis of the evidence available to us, Jesus was faithful even unto death to the messianic Judaism into which he was born and did not intend to found a new religion. It was followers and interpreters like Paul who transformed Jesus into a Savior Christ— God's chosen atoner for the sins of humankind.

In a technical sense, early Christianity was neither Trinitarian nor Unitarian. For nearly three centuries after Jesus's death, no specific doctrine of this type was enforced as part of an official Christian creed. When doctrinal controversies became too heated to contain, the Roman emperor Constantine summoned church leaders to a council at Nicaea where, in 325—almost three hundred years after the death of Jesus—the Nicene Creed was voted into existence. The godhood of Jesus thus became the official orthodoxy of the Christian religion. The Nicene formula declared, by a divided vote, that Jesus was of the same essential substance as God. It is characteristic of Unitarian Universalists, including those who retain and cherish a Christian identity, to reject the validity of the Nicene decision and to emphasize instead the symbolic and human meanings of Jesus.

A half-century later, at another gathering of church leaders, the General Council of Constantinople, the assembled dignitaries added the Holy Spirit to their formula, thus completing the Trinity. I have simplified the history, but essentially this was the very human manner in which the Trinitarian dogma of Father, Son, and Holy Spirit came into being. From the beginning, there were dedicated Christians who felt that the spiritual message and moral leadership of Jesus were being swamped in a sea of metaphysics, but it quickly became apparent that those who would not bow before the Trinitarian formula were to be expelled, condemned, and even executed for their heresy, their insistence on being able to choose.

It is worth noting that the only sources we have of the actual teachings of Jesus are the first three Gospels—Matthew, Mark, and Luke. The Gospel of John was not written to emphasize Jesus's teachings. More recent discoveries—the Gospel of Thomas, for example—add little. In their present form, Matthew, Mark, and Luke (though they contain earlier materials) were written one to two generations after Jesus's death. There is not the remotest suggestion in them of a Trinitarian formula. Indeed, Jesus—or any other Jew of his age—would have been shocked by the "blasphemy" of such a concept.

Earl Morse Wilbur, in *Our Unitarian Heritage*, writes:

> During long centuries of their national humiliation no other conviction had been so deeply burned into the conscious-

ness of the Jewish people as their belief in the absolute and unqualified oneness of God. In fact, down to this very day, nothing else has proved such an impassable barrier to the reception of Christianity by the Jews, as has the doctrine of the Trinity, which has seemed to them to undermine the very cornerstone of their religion.

It is a minor but interesting fact of Christian history that, as late as the fifth century, in an enclave east of the Jordan, a lonely handful of Jewish Christians, known as Ebionites, clung to their original beliefs in the unity of God and the pure humanity and natural birth of Jesus.

From the time of Jesus to the Council of Chalcedon, roughly 450 years, orthodox Christian doctrine, against which European Unitarianism and Universalism were eventually to protest, emerged with the belief that God, while one, exists in three persons, and that one of these persons (Jesus) has two natures (divine and human).

It is all too easy for contemporary religious freethinkers to look back on the controversies that shook the early Christian Church and conclude that centuries were spent in absurd strife over the forms rather than the substance of spiritual life. From Nicaea to Chalcedon, the councils seem to have labored mightily to bring forth vaporous verbal formulas. It must not be overlooked, however, that to Christian believers of the third and fourth centuries the very essence, and perhaps even the existence, of their faith hung on the resolutions of deep conflicts. In fairness, it must be granted that the struggles represented the emotional religious perplexities of the time. Wilbur writes:

> The character and methods of the Councils that established these doctrines are not, it is true, calculated to give us great reverence for their Christian character, nor much respect for their opinions; while the repeated interference of the civil power to enforce decisions of doctrine in its own interest was as vicious as it well could be. Yet the changes of thought . . . do not quite deserve to be called, as they often have

been, "corruptions of Christianity." No one tried, or wished to "corrupt" the Christian faith. It was, indeed, a vast change from the simple religion of the sermon on the mount and the parables of Jesus to the theology of the Nicene and Athanasian Creeds; and the whole emphasis shifted from a religion of the heart and life to abstract speculations of the head. Yet when we have made all deductions for the political intrigues and the mean jealousies and the unscrupulous ambitions that so often accompanied them, we find at the bottom of these controversies an earnest and honest desire in the best minds to state the theory of the new Christian religion in terms which the cultured old world of Greek thought could accept (*Our Unitarian Heritage*).

Anyone who has ever struggled for a cause can appreciate the fervor attached to the doctrines of the Trinity and the deity of Jesus. For early Christians their emergence was experienced as a life-and-death exertion. Once achieved, they must be defended as the essence of the Christian faith. Whoever questioned or disavowed them seemed to endanger the very soul of Christianity. It is always a temptation to identify orthodoxy with religion itself. Christians fell victim to the temptation. They came to look upon dissent as the most heinous and contemptible of crimes. Centuries later, when a few brave and enterprising spirits began to compare the creeds with the Gospels and concluded that they preferred a belief in God's unity and Jesus's humanity to the enigmas of the Trinity and the God-Man, they were fanatically attacked. The most extreme punishments—torture and burning—were considered to be no more than what these "enemies" of religion justly deserved.

Thus, through all the early history of liberal religious impulses within the Christian fold, there is a strain of violent persecution. Tragedy and death stalked those who first laid the foundations in Europe of the movement that was to bear the Unitarian and Universalist names. And it was not only the Trinity and the God-Man that were to come under critical scrutiny; other zealously guarded doctrines were also questioned. First to be challenged was

Augustine's doctrine, later elaborated by Luther and Calvin, that human nature, even in infancy, is totally corrupted by original sin. Next, another of Augustine's dogmas—a great favorite of Calvin—that Almighty God had decided at creation time which human souls to save and which to confine to eternal damnation— was denied. Finally, the notion of vicarious atonement—that Jesus provided salvation by paying for the sins of humankind—was questioned and discarded.

Thus the forerunners of Unitarianism and Universalism struck not only at the two central doctrines of orthodox Christianity, but at three derivative ones as well. From the beginning they staked the merit of their argument on a plea that the five dogmas were not only inconsistent with Scripture, but offensive to reason and the moral sense.

Nothing that could properly be called a Unitarian or Universalist movement came into existence until the Reformation was in full flow; but this does not mean that there were no pioneers of liberal religious thought prior to the sixteenth century. Such a one, for example, was Origen, born in Alexandria in C.E. 185, who was the most productive and liberal of early Christian writers and thinkers. His was a remarkably open-minded and open-ended presentation of Christianity, worthy of Erasmus, who arrived on the scene nearly 1300 years later. Origen, as a pioneer of the liberal religious tradition, richly deserves recognition not normally given to him. Soundly schooled in the science, philosophy, and theology of his time, he insisted that faith and knowledge were complementary, not antagonistic, and that religion was enriched not endangered by a rational search for truth. Absent from his makeup was the bigotry of so many of his Christian peers who were then bent on erasing the rich spiritual heritage of Greek and Stoic philosophy. He believed that the Bible was to be studied reverently but critically, and he denied that it was necessary to accept the Bible literally in all instances.

A biographer, Fred G. Bratton, writes:

> From the standpoint of charm and versatility, Origen is one of the most appealing characters in history. His independence of

mind prejudiced orthodoxy against him so that he was never beatified, but not all saints are canonized. Owing to his comparatively liberal views, the historic Christian Church has never given him his rightful place either as a thinker or as a Christian character (*The Legacy of the Liberal Spirit*).

What were some of his "comparatively liberal views"? He was the first analytical theologian. What mattered to Origen was not the confirmation of orthodox doctrines, but the fullest possible application of reasoned thought to the issues of the religious life. He was inclined to reject anything that was unreconcilable with reason. Where Tertullian would later exclaim of his Christian orthodoxy: "I believe it because it is absurd," and Augustine insisted: "I would not believe . . . if the authority of the . . . Church did not compel me," Origen consistently promoted rationality as the basis of belief.

He was a forerunner of Luther in upholding faith as the soul of the religious life, but he would have been appalled at Luther's vituperative rejection of good works. Origen saw a symbiotic relationship between faith and works, with faith rendered worthless unless expressed in ethical conduct. Throughout his writings it is the moral emphasis, as well as the celebration of reason, that stamp him as a fountainhead of the liberal tradition. By renouncing dogma, by disclaiming prejudice and ignorance, by respecting the insights of the Classical as well as the Christian world, by honoring reason, and by upholding the ethical imperatives of faith, Origen richly earned a primary place in our affection.

Another memorable but neglected figure was the English monk Pelagius, whose lifetime extended roughly from C.E. 360 to 420. His major contribution was a courageously creative advocacy of moral free will and spiritual liberty at a time when Augustine, with his insistence on the total depravity of human nature, stood astride the Christian scene like an unchallengeable colossus. Pelagius, like Origen, preached a Christian faith blessed by God with freedom of moral choice. Because Pelagius was a scholar of impressive learning and a person of undeniably honorable character, Augustine saw him as a threat to orthodoxy.

The two engaged in intense formal debates. "If I ought, I can," proclaimed Pelagius. Augustine argued back that human nature, though created upright by God, had, of its own free will, become depraved and was justly condemned to beget "a posterity in the same state of depravity and condemnation."

Dean Inge once said: "A religion succeeds, not because it is true, but because it suits its worshipers." There seems little doubt that a majority of Christians of the fifth century resonated with Augustine's enthusiasm for human depravity and condemnation. The faithful repudiated Pelagius, along with his confidence in their moral competence. One consequence was the adoption of Cyprian's doctrine, which said that in view of human depravity there could be no salvation outside the Church. Christians would wait a long time for a reassertion of the universalistic, encouraging faith of Pelagius that sin is, as he put it, "a thing of will and not of nature."

I like to think of Origen and Pelagius as bridges over which Hebrew ethical religion and Classical philosophy made their way across the stream of Christian orthodoxy into the developing liberal religion of the contemporary world. Perhaps there would have been others to do their pioneering work if they had never lived, and, in fact, there were others who would nurture the seeds of reason and moral freedom in religion, keeping them alive for the day when the climate would change and they could burst forth to challenge orthodoxy. I like to think of Origen and Pelagius as having won great, though suppressed, victories for the free human spirit. I fear that most Unitarian Universalists remain unaware of the outstanding debt owed by all liberal religionists to these two uncanonized saints of the Catholic Church.

With the ferment of the Protestant Reformation, many adventurous opportunities were opened for a more liberal spirit in religion, despite fierce opposition from such major Reformers as Luther and Calvin. Sibling to the Reformation was the Renaissance, preparer of medievalism's ultimate downfall. Revolutionary theories of the universe shattered biblical cosmology, questioned Aristotelian logic, and undermined medieval supernaturalism. The tiny sailing ships of Columbus, Magellan, and Vasco da Gama proved the earth's roundness by refusing to drop off the edge of the ocean. World trade shifted from the Adriatic to the Atlantic to the Pacific. Minds stretched to embrace new global frontiers.

Great centers of art and scholarship were created in Florence, Rome, and Augsburg. Creativity was encouraged and subsidized. Genius was celebrated, individualism honored, freedom praised. A new trust in human nature arose. Scientific exploration and the use of reason grew in luxuriant revolt against absolutism and finality.

Too little is made by biographers of Leonardo da Vinci's prophetic religious spirit. His genius as an artist and scientist is warmly recognized, but he was equally impressive as an advanced and independent thinker in religion. Deeply committed to religion as a moral rather than a creedal imperative, Leonardo was an eloquent critic of clericalism, fanaticism, superstition, and dogma. He spoke with frank disapproval, before either Erasmus or Luther, of the worship of Mary and the saints, the sale of indulgences, and the exploitation of the sacrament of confession.

He recognized the implications of the philosophical conflict between mental freedom and authoritarianism and was a solid partisan of freedom. He wrote: "When beseiged by ambitious tyrants, I find the means of defense in order to preserve the chief gift of nature which is liberty." Impatient with the church-controlled science of his time and smarting under the ban imposed on his anatomical studies, Leonardo wrote:

> Those sciences are vain and full of errors which are not born of experience, mother of all certitude, and which do not terminate in observation . . . I will make experiment before I proceed because my intention is first to set forth the facts and then to demonstrate the reason why such experience is constrained to work in such fashion. And this is the rule to be followed by the investigators of natural phenomena: while nature begins from causes and ends with experience, we must follow a contrary procedure, that is, begin from experience and with that discover the causes.

Leonardo was the best of the Renaissance spirit incarnate, a liberal mind come into being. It was the Renaissance as well as the Reformation that pointed ahead to what we Unitarian Universalists became.

The Reformation was a herald with a mixed message. Luther and Calvin replaced the authority of the Pope with that of Scripture, but left essentially unchallenged the Latin theological orthodoxy of the Church. They altered the techniques for attaining salvation, and by making Scripture rather than the Holy See the ultimate source of spiritual authority, they guaranteed a multiplicity of competing sects within the Christian world. They did not, except indirectly, encourage the life of reason in religion or cultivate a greater trust in the possibilities of human nature. They did, however, assert a priesthood of *all* believers, and by so doing opened the gates to those who would be architects of freer communions of faith.

Fourteen years after Martin Luther nailed his ninety-five theses to the Wittenberg Castle Church door, Michael Servetus startled Christendom with a furiously written book entitled *On the Errors of the Trinity*. It was an angry, strident denunciation of the dogma of the Trinity as upheld by Reformation and Catholic authorities alike. The most widely quoted of Servetus's phrases is: "Your Trinity is a product of subtlety and madness. The Gospel knows nothing of it."

The author of these no-nonsense blasphemies was nineteen years of age. His style was chaotic and intemperate, but demonstrated a remarkable range of reading and learning. The book was placed on sale in the Rhine cities and spread swiftly through Switzerland, Germany, and northern Italy. It appears that Servetus, in his youthful zeal, actually believed for a time that the major Reformers would see the light and embrace his arguments as soon as they could carefully consider them. Luther quickly quashed that hope when he labeled the book "abominably wicked." Other condemnations rose in a fierce storm.

A shaken Servetus asked to be allowed to write a second book in which he would attempt to correct the mistakes of the first. At

Basel he was given indulgence to do so. The result was a slimmer volume with the more conciliatory title *Dialogues on the Trinity*. He excised some of the objectionable passages of his earlier effort and tried to express himself in language more nearly like that of recognized Church teachers. In substance, however, he restated the vigorous dissents. Rather than pacifying his critics, he inflamed them. Lacking both friends and money, he took up medicine and disappeared from public view for more than twenty years.

A quarter of a century later, when he was on trial for his life for surfacing and reasserting his old cause, his books on the Trinity had been so successfully suppressed that not a single copy could be found for use in Calvin's court.

Martyrdom was Michael Servetus's grisly reward. Calvin had him burned at a Geneva stake after Servetus insisted, despite dire warnings, on expanding his earlier books into a new polemical work.

What alarming teachings did these volumes contain? Servetus claimed straight out that God is indivisible and that there is no Trinity taught in the Bible. Creedalisms such as Trinity, essence, and substance, he said, are inventions, foreign to Scripture. The Trinity and the doctrine of two natures in Christ actually discourage the devout from being wholehearted Christians because they are illogical, unreasonable, and contradictory. They raise unanswerable questions, lead to crises of conscience, and leave people, in effect, with no God at all. Moreover, said Servetus with missionary zeal, they are a stumbling block to the conversion of Jews and Moslems. The mission of Christianity, to spread across the face of the earth, he concluded, requires the uprooting of these doctrines.

Unitarian Origins

It is inappropriate to claim Servetus as a Unitarian. He was an anti-Trinitarian. His approach to theology was very much his own, and we honor him for that and for his courage. But he sought out no religious community of freer faith, nor did he attract one. His contribution was to give dramatic impact to the issue of dissent in

Christian thought and practice. The burning of Servetus, not by the Pope of Rome, but by the great reformer of Geneva, raised searching questions about the cruelty of religious intolerance. Castellio's memorable rebuke spoke for growing numbers: "To burn a man alive does not defend a doctrine. It slays a person."

Movements sprang up in Poland and Transylvania, which were the cradles of European Unitarianism. They were non-Trinitarian, but of greater consequence was their devotion in Christian practice to principles of spiritual liberty, reason, and tolerance. The movement in Poland was headed by the saintly, scholarly reformer Faustus Socinus. He organized liberal congregations, persuaded them to give up extreme positions, and defended them in their controversies with both Catholic and Protestant opponents. The movement spread rapidly, attracting many of the most enlightened and gifted of Poles. In spite of harsh persecution, a lasting imprint was left on Polish culture. Church records were eventually put to the torch, but it is generally believed that by 1618 there were more than three hundred Socinian congregations.

Persecution mounted under Jesuit leadership, until it became an all-out war of extermination. To the very end of their existence, the Socinians carried on an active program of education and advocacy in and beyond Poland. They were bold and enterprising in spreading their liberalized Christianity, but depended on reasoned discussion rather than impassioned crusades. They quite deliberately tried to set an example of good temper and mild speech in religious disputation and won many to their cause. In the end they went under before onslaughts of persecution. Their self-imposed moral standards were no match for the Counter-Reformation's decision to root out of Poland every vestige of the Socinian "heresy." Socinus himself was attacked in the streets of Krakow. His face was smeared and his mouth filled with mud. This was the first of a series of assaults that left him first broken, then dead.

A systematic extermination policy completely destroyed the Socinian movement in Poland. Exiles scattered over the face of

Europe: a tragic and plaintive chapter in the history of religious persecution. A few found their way to a haven in Transylvania where, for some time, there had been well-organized churches of their own type and outlook. Under the leadership of the charismatic Francis David, Transylvania had become the scene of a vital liberal Christian movement actually bearing the name *Unitarian*. It is worth noting that the label was not self-chosen. It was bestowed on Francis David's followers, as a term of vituperation, by Trinitarian critics. It stuck and assumed a life of its own. These Transylvanian liberal Christians stressed the human qualities of Jesus, the moral and spiritual teachings of Jesus, the right of congregations to choose the kind of preaching they wanted, the virtues of religious freedom and toleration. By the late sixteenth century, there were more than four hundred Unitarian congregations in the area, and they are there still. I write with special feeling about this because my wife, Joan, and I have enjoyed their warm hospitality and shared their joys and sorrows. I have preached in their churches and met with their leaders, their children, and their theological students. Four hundred years of history have bestowed on their liberal faith a remarkable maturity and steadfastness.

At the peak of his career, Francis David was Transylvania's outstanding religious figure and one of Europe's ablest preachers and theologians. Under his guidance, the only Unitarian king in history, John Sigismund of Transylvania, issued the western world's first edict of religious freedom and toleration. It read in part:

> Preachers shall be allowed to preach the Gospel everywhere, each according to his own understanding of it. If the community wish to accept such preaching, well and good; if not, they shall not be compelled, but shall be allowed to keep the preachers they prefer. No one shall be made to suffer on account of religion, since faith is the gift of God.

This bill of rights in religion marks a precious moment in Unitarian Universalist history, for it kept liberal religious faith and practice from being destroyed as it was in Poland and elsewhere.

This is not to say that Transylvanian Unitarians escaped persecution. Sigismund's successors were persuaded to adopt anti-Unitarian policies. By 1574 David's preaching and teaching were under hostile scrutiny, and within a year many of his noted followers were deprived of their rights and property. Some were tortured and mutilated; others were executed. By 1579, David was thrown into prison, where he died of exposure, hunger, and disease. Nevertheless, the spirit of religious liberty, preached by David and promulgated by Sigismund, was never completely crushed. The Unitarian congregations persisted and survived. Now part of Romania, they are tolerated but closely regulated. Once again, they need the full force of David's humane, inspiring example of unswerving loyalty to his free faith.

The saga of Unitarian pioneering in England is more merciful than on the Continent. While it is true that the first stages of the English Reformation were marked by occasional executions and frequent imprisonments, there was a gradual, if grudging, official toleration of dissent. Long before Unitarians attempted to organize themselves, capital punishment and imprisonment for religious dissidents were banished from the English scene. Civil persecutions endured, but the stake, gallows, and dungeon disappeared as deterrents to religious nonconformity.

Socinianism influenced progressive religious thinkers well into the eighteenth century. Early English Unitarians acknowledged their debt to the Polish movement by applying three principles: They advocated Socinian tolerance of differences in belief, applied the Socinian test of reason to religious doctrines, and preached the Socinian concepts of God, Jesus, and atonement.

England's developing Unitarian movement was star-studded with such notables as Isaac Newton, John Locke, Margaret Fell, John Biddle, and, for a time, William Penn. The person who most deserves credit as the actual founder of the Unitarian Church in England was Theophilus Lindsay, a Church of England cleric turned liberal. Laying aside the traditional, white surplice of his

office, Lindsay conducted the first official Unitarian service in a
London auction room. A large congregation, which included
Benjamin Franklin and Joseph Priestley, participated. The date
was April 17, 1774.

Lindsay's motivations are best understood by reviewing the
affirmations that he described as the unifying bonds of the new
Unitarian Church in England. David B. Parke quotes him:

> That there is One God, one single person, who is God, the
> sole creator and sovereign lord of all things;
>
> That the holy Jesus was a man of the Jewish nation, the
> servant of this God, highly honored and distinguished by
> him; and,
>
> That the Spirit, or Holy Spirit, was not a person, or in-
> telligent being; but only the extraordinary power or gift of
> God, imparted, first (Acts 1, 2) to our Lord Jesus Christ him-
> self, in his life-time; and afterwards, to the apostles, and
> many of the first Christians, to impower them to preach and
> propagate the gospel with success: and
>
> That this was the doctrine concerning God, and Christ,
> and the holy Spirit, which was taught by the apostles, and
> preached to jews and heathens (*Epic of Unitarianism*).

This statement would strike most of us as quaint and tangen-
tial. It is to be appreciated for the startling departure it represented
in its own age.

Coupled with Lindsay was the scientist, author, and minister
Joseph Priestley. Celebrated as the discoverer of oxygen, Priestley
was also the best known and most influential of early English
Unitarians. He gave intellectual brilliance and prodigious scholarship to the development of Unitarian religion and, together with
Lindsay, stimulated a mushrooming of Unitarian institutions. With
incredible energy, he lavished his quick mind and warm spirit on
preaching, pamphleteering, scientific research, and the espousal of
many liberal and unpopular social and political causes, including
the French Revolution. Inflamed by exasperated leaders of the

Established Church, a Birmingham mob chose Bastille Day, July 14, 1791, to attack and burn down Priestley's home, laboratory, library, and Unitarian chapel. Priestley made a hairsbreadth escape, fleeing to London, where he immediately wrote and dispatched a sermon to be read to his congregation on the following Sunday, using as his text: "Father, forgive them, for they know not what they do."

Discouraged by the prevailing political and ecclesiastical climate, and beckoned by an invitation from his friend Thomas Jefferson, he sailed, in 1794, to the United States. In Northumberland, Pennsylvania, he gathered around him the first congregation in the new nation to call itself Unitarian.

The roots of American Unitarianism were already deep by the time Priestley arrived. Liberal breezes had long been blowing through the dour Calvinism of the pre-Revolutionary colonies. Increasing numbers of ministers and laity were calling for a greater use of reason in the interpretation of Scripture, for a questioning of the doctrines of depravity and predestination, for a consideration of potential human goodness and the exercise of free moral will, and for a belief in the unity of God. Priestley's powerful presence encouraged the progress of such liberalism, but it is in figures such as Charles Chauncy, Jonathan Mayhew, and the pioneer Universalist John Murray that we should look for our Unitarian origins in America. These combined a bold humanist spirit with their Christian piety and a dauntless rationalism with their godliness. Determined at first to challenge only the dogmatism of the dominant religious institutions, the liberal leaders found themselves pressed inexorably toward a genuine break. The bonds were finally severed in the first quarter of the nineteenth century, when Unitarianism emerged as a self-consciously distinct form of organized religious life. As described by David Parke:

> Freed from the shackles of tradition and circumstance, Unitarianism embraced Unitarian Christianity, Transcendentalism, and Naturalism in such rapid succession that the radicalism of Boston in 1819 was the conservatism of Cambridge in 1838 and anachronism of Chicago in 1880. Unitarianism

also became the mind and pen of America as the Nation sought to discover where she was, where she had been, and where she was going. It was a magnificent century, one, like those of Jesus and Luther, to be relived and ploughed back into the future (*Epic of Unitarianism*).

Two colossi of the "magnificent century" were William Ellery Channing and Theodore Parker. Each could boast of sturdy Yankee and Revolutionary lineage. The first Channing came to the colonies from Dorsetshire, England, in 1711, and the Parkers were residents of Lexington, Massachusetts, for nearly two centuries before Theodore was born. Each had one foot firmly planted in New England morality and the other foot in the Enlightenment's rationalism. Both were prodigious readers and scholars. Both were forceful preachers.

Channing achieved his religious liberalism through an evolution from Calvinist training and belief. In his youth he believed that God had elected from the beginning those who would be saved and those who would be damned, and that human nature (including his own) was sunk in hopeless depravity. In maturity he believed that God bestows love upon all. His espousal of Unitarianism was determined by a growing conviction that human nature is endowed with an intrinsic moral sense that gives the power to perceive and choose good. Short, slight, supremely self-disciplined, Channing projected an image of humility, intellectuality, compassion, moral strength, social vision, and natural leadership. His only ministry, from 1803 to 1842, was in Boston's Federal Street Church (later relocated and renamed Arlington Street Church). It proved to be a succession of great events. In his book-lined study were organized not only the American Unitarian Association, but new societies for the promotion of world peace, early childhood and adult education, social work and ministries to the poor, prison reform, care for the mentally ill, and temperance. He became one of the most prestigious voices raised against slavery and for abolition. Nothing was more compelling to Channing than the defense and enhancement of human dignity. He worked to rouse New England and the nation from the comas of Calvinism and materialism. He felt that religious leaders had become priestly rather than prophetic, while for many of the laity the real god was commerce. He was determined to stir the spiritual imagination, light a fire of moral responsibility, and make the living of a life greater than the making of a living.

Using writing desk, pulpit, and lecture platform as tools, he had an astonishing influence in three major areas: the liberalization of theology, the implementation of social reform, and the stimulation of a literary and cultural renaissance. Not the least of his accomplishments was to give emotional support and practical encouragement to a vanguard of empowerment-bent women, including Dorothea Dix, Elizabeth Peabody, Lydia Maria Child, and Margaret Fuller.

It is now hard to believe that *any* sermon could create the stir that Channing's Baltimore address did at the ordination of Jared Sparks in 1819. Yet, nearly every leading Unitarian minister made the exhausting horse-drawn journey to be present. Thousands of copies of the sermon were prepared in advance for immediate circulation. Like Luther's Wittenberg theses, Channing's statements at Baltimore were destined to compel people to take a stand on fundamental religious issues.

Channing scored orthodox theology for according humans no freedom but that of being damned or saved by an arbitrary God. In the Baltimore address he called this an insult both to God and to humans. He went on to object strongly "to the contemptuous manner in which human reason is often spoke of by our adversaries. . . . We indeed grant, that the use of reason in religion is accompanied with danger. But we ask any honest person to look upon the history of the Church, and say, whether the renunciation of it is not still more dangerous."

Turning to his belief in the unity and benevolence of God, Channing said:

> We cannot bow before a being, however great and powerful, who governs tyrannically. We respect nothing but excellence, whether on earth or in heaven. We venerate, not the loftiness

of God's throne, but the equity and goodness in which it is established. We believe that God is infinitely good, kind, benevolent, in the proper sense of these words; good in disposition, as well as in act; good not to a few, but to all; good to every individual, as well as to the general system.

Trying to summarize Channing's influence is like trying to summarize an epoch. Perhaps he did it best himself when he wrote:

> I have lost no occasion for expressing my deep attachment to liberty in all its forms, civil, political, religious; to liberty of thought, speech and the press, and of giving utterance to my abhorrence of all forms of oppression.

If Channing was the most influential figure yet produced by American Unitarianism, Theodore Parker was the most remarkable. At the height of his preaching career in Boston's Music Hall, he spoke Sunday after Sunday to congregations of three thousand or more. His grandfather, Lexington's Captain John Parker, had delivered himself of one of the Revolution's immortal phrases, when in 1775 he said of the advancing British: "If they mean to have a war, let it begin here." Years later, when Parker made up his mind to defy the Fugitive Slave Law, he recalled his grandfather's famous words and wrote:

> I have had to arm myself. I have written my sermons with a pistol in my desk—loaded, a cap on the nipple, and ready for action. This I have done in Boston, in the midst of the 19th century; been obliged to do it to defend the innocent members of my church, women as well as men. You know I do not like fighting . . . but what could I do? I was born in the little town where the first bloodshed of the Revolution began. My grandfather drew the first sword in the Revolution. With these memories in me, when a parishioner, a fugitive from slavery, a woman, pursued by kidnappers, came to my house, what could I do less than take her in and defend her to the last? (*Epic of Unitarianism*).

Parker made religion more than an ecclesiastical exercise. He took it from the pulpit onto the highways and into the cities and towns of expanding America. This is literally true in terms of his Herculean lecture tours, and figuratively true by reason of the subjects over which his mind and pen ranged. He was a pathfinder in the practical applications of religion and a trailblazer in confronting secular issues with spiritual standards. He was, Henry Steele Commager wrote in his preface to Parker's *Yankee Crusader*,

> the conscience of the North—of such men as Charles Sumner and John Hale and Abraham Lincoln, and of countless thousands of ordinary men and women who were troubled by the contrast between the faith they professed and the practices they tolerated.

To Parker, there were no exemptions from the imperatives of moral law; getting from Sunday to Monday, from the observances of religion to the practice of religion in every kind of human relationship, was the real business of the church. He recognized no compartmentalizing of the spiritual from the secular. To him they were one, and human beings were bound, if their faith be true, to be deeply involved in correcting the injustices of the political, commercial, and social order.

His ministry began in West Roxbury, Massachusetts, where he promised his congregation "to preach nothing as religion that I have not experienced inwardly and made my own." Many hours were spent in the well-stocked libraries for which Boston was noted. He nurtured his mind, ministered devotedly to the seventy families of his congregation, wrote essays and articles for transcendentalist publications, and took an active interest in the affairs of the nearby Utopian Brook Farm community. Then came Emerson's Harvard Divinity School Address:

> Historic Christianity has fallen into the error that corrupts all attempts to communicate religion. As it appears to us, and as it has appeared for ages, it is not the doctrine of the

soul, but an exaggeration of the personal, the positive, the ritual. It has dwelt, it dwells, with noxious exaggeration about the person of Jesus. The soul knows no persons. It invites (all) to expand to the full circle of the universe, and will have no preferences but those of spontaneous love.

Parker was stirred and depressed. Emerson's repudiation of miracles, his human-centered sovereignty of spirit, his celebration of "moral science" thrilled Parker. But Emerson had turned his back on the Unitarian parish ministry and sought other channels for his talents and energies. Parker brooded over whether the ministry was a wide enough place for him and decided that it was. He would remain in the pulpit and do everything in his power to make the church an instrument for the very things he and Emerson wanted.

By moving into downtown Boston, Parker gained a national platform at the Twenty-Eighth Congregational Society. His sermons recognized the profound revelations taking place in science and philosophy. They were circulated, read, and discussed from one end of the country to the other, and in Europe as well. Like Emerson, he insisted that miracles proved nothing about religion. The permanent truths of the spiritual life are confirmed by experience and practice. The forms of Christianity change, the substance of religion remains. "If it could be proved," he said in a sermon entitled "The Transient and Permanent in Christianity," "that the gospels were a fabrication and that Jesus of Nazareth never lived, Christianity would still stand firm and fear no evil." Scientific truths do not rest on the word of their discoverer. Gravity does not operate because Newton said so. The same is true of the truths of religion. Confirm them by experience, and not by whether Jesus spoke them, or the Bible records them, or doctrine upholds them!

No part of my legacy as a Unitarian Universalist minister is more precious to me than the portion created by Theodore Parker. He was a prophet of righteousness, justice, and mercy who believed, as I do, in the progressive development of the church. "The

church," he wrote, "should be the means of reforming the world.
. . . It should therefore bring up the ideas of the times, the sentiments of the times and the actions of the times, and judge them
by the universal standard."

Parker scandalized many of his Unitarian colleagues, just as
Emerson did, and strenuous efforts were made to expel him from
the Unitarian ministry. It was a time for many of the more cau-
tious Unitarians to attempt appeasement of the orthodox. Parker's
outspokenness was an embarrassment. It was, for me, a godsend
to succeeding generations. Parker was the wave of the future for
the kind of Unitarianism that could attract and hold the likes of
me. It is his spirit that has prevailed sufficiently to preserve a genius for which liberal religion is especially suited—a genius that
he himself described: "Progressive development does not end with
us; we have seen only the beginnings; the future triumphs must be
vastly greater than all accomplished yet."

The Universalists

There is one terror I would banish from every heart in the world
if I could: the fear of hell. In the early years of my ministry, I was
asked by a couple who were strangers to me if I would conduct a
funeral service for a family member. I listened, shaken, as they described their last experience with death, the death of a baby born
to close relatives. The officiating minister felt compelled by his
doctrinal belief to announce that the infant was burning in hell
because she had died unbaptized. With all due respect for the sincerity of that minister's belief in infant damnation, I felt then, as I
feel now, that for anyone to make a statement like that to grief-
stricken parents is not only incredibly cruel but also the opposite
of all that I hold to be religious.

Were this an isolated case we might sadly let it pass, but with
the passing years I have been approached over and over again in
similar circumstances because it was known that I did not believe
in hell and would not use a funeral as an occasion to harrow grief.

To their everlasting credit, our Universalist forebears were lifting their voices aginst the cruel myth of hell as early as the last half of the eighteenth century. In England and in the American colonies, brave spirits began to preach that it was unthinkable for God, as a loving creator-parent, to damn any of God's children everlastingly to hell. How could the offspring of a good God be willfully consigned to damnation by that same God? The creedal assumptions formulated at Nicaea must be in error. Even though the Nicaean Council had pointed out that God's justice *required* the punishment of sin, it was self-evident that a good and perfect God created humans to grow eternally in the goodness of their creator.

In the 1740s these "heretical" notions were preached in Pennsylvania by George de Benneville, a scholar and physician, born in England of Protestant French parents, members of the nobility. After his parents' death, he was taken under the wing of his godmother, Queen Anne of England. She appointed him midshipman in the Royal Navy when he was twelve. He later was educated at the University of Padua and at seventeen, in France, was converted to Universalism. For preaching unconventional religious views, he was imprisoned and tried for treason. Sentenced to death, he was, at the last moment, reprieved. In 1741, at the age of thirty-eight, and by invitation of Christopher Sower, a Universalist Quaker, he arrived in Philadelphia, where booksellers were already displaying Universalist writings. He established his home near Reading, Pennsylvania, and used one room as a chapel and a day school for a newly gathered Universalist congregation of fifty.

In the 1760s, in England, the espousal of Universalist ideas brought about the excommunication of John Murray, a zealous lay teacher and preacher of Methodism and a familiar of John Wesley, George Whitefield, and other pioneers of that movement. Murray was successful in business, married, and the father of an infant. Through the influence of James Relly of London, Murray became a convinced Universalist. He must have wondered about the wisdom of his conversion. His seemingly solid life fell apart. Death took his wife and child; his business failed; he was imprisoned for debt. By the time he won his release, he was in a deep depression. He resolved to bury himself in what he thought of as the wilderness of America and never to preach again.

Through a series of circumstances, which he ever after believed to be providential, he found himself strolling in 1770 along the New Jersey shore near Barnegat Bay, where he had arrived as the captain of a small vessel that he had promised to sail to New York as soon as the wind permitted. A stranger named Thomas Potter approached Murray and said: "The wind will never change, sir, until you have delivered to us, in that meeting house, a message from God." Potter, a local settler with strong, unconventional religious views, had constructed a meetinghouse but had been unable to find a minister to his taste. There was no change in the wind. Murray yielded to Potter's persuasion. He preached. Still gun-shy from his earlier experience, he preached what he thought of as a crypto-Universalist sermon. No matter. The wind changed in more ways than one, and Murray became something of an instant celebrity. Soon there were invitations from up and down the East Coast, including Gloucester, Massachusetts, where Murray settled as a minister of a small Universalist group and met Judith Sargent, a young widow, who became his second wife.

Judith Sargent Murray, member of a prominent Massachusetts family, was both a Universalist who proclaimed the final harmony of all human souls with God and a vivid, vital early feminist. Her essay, *On the Equality of the Sexes*, published in 1790 in *The Massachusetts Magazine*, is an extraordinary manifesto, in which she declares:

> Yes, ye lordly, ye haughty sex, our souls are by nature *equal* to yours; the same breath of God animates, enlivens, and invigorates us; and that we are not fallen lower than yourselves, let those witness who have greatly towered above the various discouragements by which they have been so heavily oppressed.

George de Benneville and the Murrays are among the most deservedly revered of those who established the Universalist movement on this continent, but their coworkers, often very ordinary and unassuming folks, made of early Universalism a genuine enterprise of common people, buoyed by the faith that the love of God will ultimately prevail over human sinfulness. They were certain of this because they believed the love of God to be the most powerful force in the universe.

The Calvinist majority was understandably disturbed by such perilous wandering from sound doctrine. It was expected from arrogant Unitarians, but this was a threat from a new quarter. There was immediate denunciation of the Universalists as an errant and irresponsible lot bent on encouraging loose lives of wickedness, in the deluded belief that no matter what they did, they could count on escaping the torments of hell. They are free thinkers and godless misinterpreters of a just God, said the Calvinist accusers, no better than Unitarians! In many towns and villages, children were sternly instructed by their pastors and parents not to look a known Universalist in the eye lest Satan lay a curse upon them.

Bracing themselves against the storm of abuse, Universalists steadfastly defended the moral character of God, insisting that God is by nature loving, rational, and redemptive. Sin, they said, is finite (reminiscent of Pelagius). Punishment is remedial, not vindictive. A future of social humanism and humanitarianism in Universalist development was forecast by this early emphasis on the ethical and redemptive aspects of God's nature, and therefore of religious living.

The movement grew slowly, for the tempest of vilification was so strong that as late as 1800 only a handful of churches had been formed. Then there appeared on the New England scene a rebel preacher and self-taught theologian of outstanding ability. His name was Hosea Ballou, and he was a courageous, scholarly, and eloquently persuasive Universalist leader. He was born and reared a Calvinistic Baptist on a small Richmond, New Hampshire, farm. Somewhere along the line he was impressed with the "awful doctrine," as Universalism was called, and began to ride the circuit, preaching the universal salvation of all of God's children. Dressed in homespun, the tall, athletic Ballou made a strong impression on admirers and critics alike. His sermons were peppered with wit and earthy stories of the land and its people. The like-minded loved his humor. Those offended by his theology thought he was bitter and sarcastic. A well-remembered anecdote illustrates why. In a discussion period following one of his sermons, he was angrily challenged: "What would you do with a man who died reeking in sin and crime?" "I think it would be a good plan to bury him," he answered.

The year 1803 was a lively one for Ballou and the struggling Universalist movement. At the Universalist General Convention of 1802, a committee including Ballou had been appointed to draw up a plan of faith and fellowship for Universalists. The move was controversial because of prevalent opposition among Universalists to "human creeds," though Articles of Faith had been adopted by a Universalist convention in Philadelphia in 1790. Strong feelings about creeds were running when the 1803 convention met in Winchester, New Hampshire.

The Winchester Profession, as it came to be known, was adopted, but only after vigorous debate and adoption of an amendment allaying fears that the profession might one day be used as an instrument of oppression or exclusion. The document emphasized standard Universalist views of God's universal love and the example and leadership of Jesus. It represented not only a further rupture with orthodoxy, but a departure from some of John Murray's tenets. Murray held orthodox beliefs about atonement and Christ's role as divine atoner.

For Ballou, the Winchester Profession served as a starting point for views that he progressively expanded. In 1805, he published his celebrated *Treatise on the Atonement*, in which he effectively demolished atonement as a Universalist concept. He greatly expanded the idea of a loving God. Christ is not God, he said, but God's messenger of love and reconciliation. He added the phrase "salvation by character." As for the punishment of sin, he stated that it was instantaneous, constant, and inevitable, but it was not

everlasting, for the self-evident reason that everlasting punishment makes no sense. Unless punishment has character for its
purpose, it is vicious and cruel. The only defensible reason for
punishment is growth in righteousness. He asked: "Is God any less
intelligent than any parent? Would a parent see any point in punishing a child forever? Would that improve the child?"

Ballou made a statement that was as Unitarian as any of his
time. His thought resembled Channing's to a remarkable degree,
with the added luster that it anticipated many of the things
Channing would say only in subsequent years. Most of the
Universalist congregations and ministers followed Ballou's lead,
making their movement an organized Unitarian Universalist
movement fifteen to twenty years before Unitarians, as such, gave
themselves official form.

Sadly, there was never any enthusiasm among emerging
Unitarian leaders for close ties with embattled Universalists. One
might assume that when Ballou, clearly a leading light of
Universalism, came to Boston in 1817 to minister to a major
Universalist congregation on School Street, he might have been embraced by the Unitarians as an ally. Instead, he was coldly ignored.
Unitarians were afraid of being bracketed with Universalists by the
orthodox. Their heretical views of Christ's nature were radical
enough; God forbid that they be labeled universal salvationists as
well. From 1815 to 1840, as Unitarians were seceding from
Calvinists and Calvinists were repudiating Unitarians, the
Universalists, whose cause was virtually identical on the issues
involved, looked longingly for encouragement, cooperation, understanding, and fellowship from Unitarians. Universalism did not
possess the social and cultural status of Unitarianism, and rein-
forcement was desperately needed. It was not forthcoming.

The situation pained Hosea Ballou, who wrote a poignant sermon addressed to Unitarians. He selected the pertinent text,
"Nevertheless, I have somewhat against thee." He wrote eloquently
of the affinity of the two groups. He rehearsed their common aspirations and frustrations and called for an intellectual and spiritual

unity. He chided Unitarians for currying favor with groups much less friendly to Unitarian ideas, while snubbing Universalism. Many of us who patiently pressed for the merger of the two bodies, which at long last took place, felt that Hosea Ballou's spirit smiled upon our efforts. One of my favorite anecdotes about him is the following.

On a preaching engagement, he arrived at the home where he was to be put up and was greeted by his hostess, who had mop in hand.

"This is Mr. Ballou, I suppose?"

"Yes, madam. My name is Ballou."

"Well, Mr. Ballou, they say you hold that all will be saved. Do you really believe that doctrine?"

"Yes, madam. I really believe it."

"Why sir! Do you really believe that all are going to be saved just such creatures as they are?"

Seeing that she did not understand the nature of salvation as he understood it, Ballou asked: "What is that you have in your hand, dear woman?"

"Why it is my mop."

"Your mop? Well, what are you going to do with it?"

"I am going to mop up my floor. I always do it on Saturday afternoon."

"Well, sister, I understand you. Are you going to mop it up just as it is?"

"Mop it up just as it is?"

"Yes, you wished to know if I hold that all will be saved just as they are. Do you intend to mop up the floor just as it is?"

"Why, I mop it up to clean it."

"True. You do not require it to be made clean before you will consent to mop it up. God saves us to purify us; that's what salvation is designed for. God does not require us to be pure in order to save us."

During the latter part of the nineteenth century, Universalism, like Unitarianism, was deeply stirred by the rise of critical biblical scholarship and studies in evolution. As Max A. Kapp described:

Darwinianism (from 1859 on) posed a challenge to all Bible-centered faith: Universalism . . . not without pangs, accepted the implications of the theory of evolution and other scientific findings. . . . A marked shift of emphasis has gradually taken place so that "salvation" no longer suggests to most Universalists an event in the after-life, but a process of self-fulfillment and social transformation.

As late as 1899 a Universalist statement of faith adopted in Boston read: "We believe in the Bible as containing a revelation from God." But by 1955 a profession approved in Washington stated: "We avow our faith in the authority of truth, known or to be known." It is impossible to miss the broadening of view inherent in these statements.

In this century the same degree of theological diversity developed among Universalists as among Unitarians. There were theists, humanists, naturalists, and mystics. There were Universalists who retained a loyal, albeit liberal, identification with Christianity, and Universalists who chose not to be known as Christians. All Universalists came to accept what they called the liberty clause, which meant simply that no creedal test might be used for determining who should or should not be a Universalist.

I am deeply fond of the Universalist name. The Unitarian name is precious to me both personally and historically. But simply as a word, laying aside for a moment the aura of history, it does not possess the magnificent, contemporary fitness of *Universalism*. It was a bit awesome, as we moved toward the merger of our faiths to contemplate calling ourselves Unitarian Universalists or Universalist Unitarians, but I warmly favored retaining both names and am content with the designation that was adopted—the Unitarian Universalist Association.

When the historic merger of 1961 finally took place, it united more than six hundred Unitarian congregations with nearly four hundred Universalist congregations. Since both bodies had what is called congregational polity, there was no change of governance at the local level. *Congregational polity* simply means that the seat of authority is in the local church or fellowship, rather than in a synod, presbytery, or bishopric. It is the democratic town-meeting principle in action in religion.

I look back with satisfaction on my warm support of the merger. Its overall result has been to strengthen the free church in its fundamental tasks. The liberal church should be one of the most contemporary and realistic of institutions. It should seek every legitimate means to rationalize and invigorate its internal administration. Combining the supplementary and complementary energies of Unitarians and Universalists was a logical move in this direction. The broader our base of human resources, the more likely it is that we will do an effective job of imparting creative moral inspiration to people's lives. The greater the invasions of freedom and civil liberty in the larger society, the more urgent it is to cherish and enlarge the practice of freedom in smaller religious communities. Obviously, this cannot happen by accident. Intelligent planning and wise organization are required. In today's world, freedom is threatened by assault and adulteration, but it is also weakened by prosaic institutional arrangements. The merger of Universalists and Unitarians was an imaginative venture, in keeping with progressive approaches to institutional life. It enlarges our horizons and invigorates the general climate of liberal religion.

The vital role of the liberal church is one of leavening. We must be the yeast of spiritual liberty that is forever working and increasing. We must be bearers and breeders of freedom. For us, denominational arrangements are not matters of authority but effective implementations of the services we require and the causes we espouse. Authority does not inhere in structures themselves, but only in the consistency and adequacy of evidence in any proposal or proposition and in demonstrations of character and competence on the part of persons charged with leadership responsibilities. Thus titles and positions bestow no automatic power. Free men and women do not bow before offices. Respect is not accorded to positions as such. For the sake of the creative uses of freedom, we devise bylaws, boards, committees, offices, and positions. These are established, not to restrict, limit, or circumscribe freedom, but to enable us to reach out beyond present customs and boundaries into unexplored realms, and to do so with maximum effectiveness. This requires maturity, not only in individuals, but in the techniques of planning and implementing. The democratic process is of great importance to us. The institution must grow in depth and breadth, along with the people who comprise it.

The history of the merger is an engaging tale of triumph over many tribulations. For more than a century the two groups grew increasingly, albeit warily, conscious of one another. Their separate histories are notched with efforts to effect a closer relationship. There are also long-standing grievances. Tufts College, for example, owes its beginnings to Universalists who were devoted to providing higher education free of creedal tests. But these founders made no secret of their wish to establish a first-rank college as an alternative to Unitarian-dominated Harvard. They did not want their Universalist youth subjected to the snobbishness and elitism of Harvard's Unitarians.

On more than a dozen occasions resolutions were introduced calling for some kind of union of the two movements. Somehow, the practicalities of getting together dampened whatever ardor there was. In 1899 a motion adopted by both bodies established a joint committee to "seek coordination—not consolidation; unity, not union." There were no notable results. In 1908 a National Federation of Religious Liberals was established. It was, on paper, a considerable coup, for the membership was to include not only Unitarians and Universalists, but Quakers and the Central Conference of American Rabbis. Alas, little came of the effort. In 1923 Universalists were courted by the National Convention of Congregational Churches, and each group appointed a Committee on Comity and Unity. Four foot-dragging years later, the Universalist Committee met with an interested group of Unitarians to discuss setting up a Congregational-Universalist-Unitarian organization, but the whole movement fell through. By 1933 still another council was incorporated in Massachusetts, known as the Free Church of America. Nearly one hundred Universalist and Unitarian congregations affiliated, along with one Methodist church, one independent church, and three Community churches. It was never possible to raise enough money for either a staff or a program (the word *free* was apparently interpreted in a financial as well as a spiritual sense), so the movement withered.

In 1947 a joint Universalist-Unitarian commission was established to lay the groundwork for federal union, and after an overwhelmingly favorable plebiscite among all member congregations of both bodies, the commission was instructed to draw up and present a practical plan. By 1951 the commission was ready to recommend an immediate union in religious education, publications, and public relations, with a gradual trend toward a complete merger. The report was ratified by both bodies, and the Council of Liberal Churches (Universalist-Unitarian) was organized in 1953. Meanwhile, the youth groups of the two bodies voted to dissolve their separate structures and merge. The result was Liberal Religous Youth, since reorganized and renamed Young Religious Unitarian Universalists. Just as the merger seemed to be an untroubling enterprise for youth, so it was for religious educators, who, from the first days of the Council of Liberal Churches, proceeded to work smoothly together across all previous denominational lines. The recommendation was then made and accepted that a commission be set up to bring the question of a complete merger to a head.

In May 1960, in Boston, by overwhelming vote, the two denominational structures became one.

Christian or More Than Christian?

> All creatures weak or strong,
> Great or small
> Seen or unseen,
> Near or far,—
> May all be blessed with peace.
> Let all-embracing thoughts
> For all that lives be thine.
>
> SUTTA-NIPATA

I have blocked out where I was when in 1982 I first heard the news that the Israeli army, navy, and air force were attacking Lebanon with the suddenness and violence of a tornado. I remember the chills that ran up my spine. To me, this was personal. Over the years, I had spent many days and nights becoming acquainted with the men, women, and children—Israeli, Lebanese, Palestinian, Jewish, Christian, Moslem—who were once again caught in a terrible web of slaughter and destruction. I had recently, in the company of Jesse Jackson, sat down with political and religious leaders of Israel, with Lebanon's major factions, and with the Palestine Liberation Organization. We had listened to their grievances, rages, and fears and pleaded with them to find a different way; to break out of their desperate cycle of pain; to give up military "solutions," armed struggle, terrorism; to sit down, in mutual recognition, at the bargaining table.

My life has been rich with opportunities to make junkets of this kind, to meet with, mingle with, and write about the peoples of the world in all of their luxuriant diversity. My respect for this diversity has grown deep, along with my horror at the brutalizing intolerance one faith seems to breed against another faith. All over the globe, the religious beliefs and aspirations of people empower their determination to achieve a better life. All over that same globe, these same religious beliefs and aspirations breed violence and vengeance.

What is a Unitarian Universalist's approach to the world's vast pattern of religions? Has liberal religion grown beyond its Judeo-Christian cradle and become something more universal? Or is it a unique expression of a Christianity that views without prejudice or missionary yearnings the spiritual traditions of others?

When the Unitarian Universalist Association was formed in 1961, the principles to which it was dedicated were these:

> Support the free and disciplined search for truth as the foundation of religious fellowship;
>
> Cherish and spread the universal truths taught by the great prophets and teachers of humanity in every age and tradition, immemorially summarized in the Judeo-Christian heritage as love to God and love to humankind;
>
> Affirm, defend, and promote the supreme worth and dignity of every human personality, and the use of the democratic method in human relationships;
>
> Implement the vision of one world by striving for a world community founded on ideals of brotherhood [*sic*], justice, and peace (UUA bylaws).

True to our penchant for self-examination, we have spent recent years in a denomination-wide exploration of fresh ways to state our principles, taking special note of the concerns of the UUA Women and Religion Committee and the UU Women's

Federation. A new statement of principles, now before us for final adoption at the 1985 General Assembly, reads as follows:

> We, the member congregations of the Unitarian Universalist Association, covenant to affirm and promote:
> - The inherent worth and dignity of every person;
> - Justice, equity and compassion in human relations;
> - Acceptance of one another and encouragement to spiritual growth in our congregations;
> - A free and responsible search for truth and meaning;
> - The rights of conscience and the use of democratic process within our congregations and in society at large;
> - The goal of world community with peace, liberty and justice for all;
> - Respect for the interdependent web of all existence of which we are a part.
>
> The living tradition we share draws from many sources:
> - Direct experience of that transcending mystery and wonder, affirmed in all cultures, which moves us to a renewal of the spirit and an openness to the forces which create and uphold life;
> - Words and deeds of prophetic women and men which challenge us to confront powers and structures of evil with justice, compassion, and the transforming power of love;
> - Wisdom from the world's religions which inspires us in our ethical and spiritual life;
> - Jewish and Christian teachings which call us to respond to God's love by loving our neighbors as ourselves;
> - Humanistic teachings which counsel us to heed the guidance of reason and the results of science, and warn us against idolatries of the mind and spirit.
>
> Grateful for the religious pluralism which enriches and ennobles our faith, we are inspired to deepen our understanding and expand our vision. As free congregations we

enter into this covenant, promising to one another our mutual trust and support.

This new statement is certainly wordier, but it is also remarkably inclusive. It could not be otherwise, considering the many currents that run strong in our movement. It is an urgent reminder to ourselves of our world's need for a new approach to faith, one that feeds the hungers of the human spirit without asking us to divide into hostile sects or split our minds into segments. The absence of such a faith—a faith expressed in the idiom of our age, at peace with its scientific method, awakening a real and deep interest in the soul, appealing to the highest and profoundest sentiments of our nature, permeating every facet of our being, and directing its enormous powers into channels that are creative and uniting—is a great spiritual tragedy in our troubled world. I could not remain within the Unitarian Universalist fold unless I felt that we were genuinely striving to build and exemplify such a faith.

A significant minority within our ranks deeply cherish their Christian identity. Organized in the Unitarian Universalist Christian Fellowship, they keep warmly alive in our midst an appreciation of our Christian roots and a reverence for the life and teachings of Jesus. I rejoice in this, just as I do in the lively identity maintenance cultivated by Unitarian Universalists for Jewish Awareness. I am willing to call myself a Christian and a Jew, but only if in the next breath I am permitted to say that in varying degrees I am also a Hindu, a Moslem, a Buddhist, a Humanist, a Stoic, and an admirer of Akhenaton, Zoroaster, Confucius, Laotze, Simone de Beauvoir, and Black Elk.

Channing was thinking only of Christianity when he said: "We must shun the spirit of sectarianism as from hell. We must shudder at the thought of shutting up God in any denomination." I, as a present-day Unitarian Universalist, would extend the sentiment to include all the world's religions. Overwhelmingly, the organized faiths, from Christianity to communism, still remain bastions of the tense, closed, heresy-hunting mind. I cannot choose for others, but I can choose for myself. I can give my loyalty to a religious community whose aim is to unite the universal sources of divine-human inspiration. For me such a community must shun the spirit of sectarianism and shudder at the thought of shutting up God.

There are dangers in this approach, and not those imagined by the many determined souls, usually anonymous, who have tried over the years, by postal service and telephone, to save my soul because I do not accept the exclusive saviorship of Christ. The dangers I have in mind inhere in any reach that may exceed our grasp. What I and most of my coreligionists are striving to achieve can easily become a leaky bucket for sloppy thinking. It can be a way of avoiding genuine issues in aimless and untested benevolence. It is easy, at a distance, to build illusions about the other great religions. We are close enough to Christianity and Judaism to be realistic about their excesses, egotisms, and dogmatisms, but when we speak of the far-away faiths, particularly Eastern ones, our voices tend to take on hushed tones; our eyes acquire a starry glow; our worship services dwell sentimentally on Zen, Krishna, and Taoist poetry. Somehow we are not impressed that exotic faiths also have their excesses, egotisms, and dogmatisms. We are understandably upset about Christian encroachments on public schools, legislatures, courts, and abortion rights, or Jewish encroachments on the rights of Palestinians, but we are somehow much less alert to invasions, often violent, into the lives of peoples in Moslem, Buddhist, or Hindu lands.

It is very attractive for us to think of ourselves as a bridge for the world's religions. After all, we have no exclusionary myths to defend, no creeds to enforce. We are open to all that is ethically best in the world's religions, and through freedom, reason, and tolerance, we feel prepared to touch each of the great faiths sympathetically and draw together their moral teachings. It is a grave mistake, however, to view this as a superficial task. Most of the hungry, diseased, and superstition-ridden folk—and they are the vast majority of the world's peoples—haven't the vaguest idea what we are talking about. I am only saying that it is extremely important for us to know what we are talking about.

We speak over and over again of our acceptance of change, and we are properly critical of those who resist change. Yet the kind of change we know and understand is comparatively mild and orderly. There are vast areas of the world where change, when it comes, is like a volcano. It erupts with formidable fury. Most of us have known very little of that kind of change.

When the General Assembly of the Unitarian Universalist Association met in Boston in June 1969, it found itself faced with a nerve-shattering schism over black empowerment, from which we are still trying to recover. In the middle 1960s, there was broad support in our ranks for the civil rights movement led by Martin Luther King. In keeping with a growing militancy among black civil rights activists, Unitarian Universalist blacks formed a Black Unitarian Universalist Caucus, recruited a cadre of white supporters, of whom I was one, and confronted our movement with a series of racial justice demands, including special funding and black leadership for an aggressive denominational assault on racism, our own, as well as that of the larger society. At the General Assembly in Cleveland in June 1968, the demands of the caucus were approved by a two-thirds majority vote, but there were deep lacerations.

As the Commission on Appraisal (1984) described in a report:

> The black empowerment issue hit the Unitarian Universalists particularly hard. . . . The issue was especially painful . . . because, as primarily middle-class whites who make democratic practice an exercise in religion and who are proud of their traditions of social progress, hearing that they are a racist church compounded a guilt they already felt for not having more members of color.

By 1969, in Boston, the guilt, for many, had turned into resentment. Continued funding for the Black Affairs Council barely survived. In 1970, it ended amid waves of stress, anger, and disillusionment and the dwindling of blacks from denominational involvement.

Perceptions of why we botched the test of black empowerment will probably always vary widely. The confrontational tactics of the Black Caucus made sense to those who used them because, out of their experience, they truly believed it was the only way their needs would be understood and addressed. While some of us whites could identify with that, many could not. The abrasive strategy of "demands," even though for a genuine transfer of power to black leadership, was traumatically offensive to the way we normally did business. As the Commission on Appraisal report put it: "Those who are not oppressed must overcome their own preconceptions in order truly to side with the oppressed." This did not happen. To me a great opportunity was lost. We were confronted with a demand for change that came upon us with a fierce, unfamiliar passion. Since there is enough fault to spread around liberally, finger pointing is absurd. It is my sense, not without foundation, that we are experiencing the rise of fresh corporate responses to the issue of racism as a compelling priority.

But to return to our desire to play a universalizing role in the world community of faiths, I again emphasize the pitfalls of romanticizing the task. We must be careful how we tread in areas that are not very real to our experience, like the late 1960s' thrust for black empowerment. It would be a sobering error to assume that we of the Western Unitarian Universalist movement are now prepared to live in the world community. We are not. At the most rudimentary level, the unvarnished sights, sounds, smells, passions, and credulities of the vast bulk of the world's peoples would certainly frighten and perhaps sicken us if we were thrown suddenly into their midst.

What we do have to our credit is an honest desire to play a useful, constructive, and uniting role. We will learn soon enough that some of our notions about spiritual unity and global religious fellowship are realizable only in part, over long periods of time, and as a result of infinite patience. Basically, ours is a nature that seeks peace and pursues it. We will develop a more agonized appreciation of how unreal peace can seem to the emaciated parents of starving children who have been exploited. We will increasingly discover that world community is not an abstraction about which we can make inspiring poems, but a fearsome concreteness of honesty and corruption, cleanliness and filth, kindness and barbarism, hope and hunger, ballots and bullets. This consciousness is growing in us, and we are right to cultivate it, because the world community is a reality and we must begin to treat it as such. We will become better, stronger people than we are—sadder and wiser. We will make more room in our hearts and minds for tragedy, because widespread tragedy is one of the hallmarks of the present world community, and total tragedy could become its end result.

We will not desert our humanism. Instead, it will become sturdier and more reliable because it learns to accept the very real presence of despair in people's lives. We will not forsake our optimism, but it will become a chastened optimism based more on our human ability to transcend error and cruelty than on the possibility of completely abolishing them.

Like all others on the North American continent, we religious liberals live in the shadow of colossal United States military and economic power which, much of the time, seems incredibly deficient in ideas of how to nourish the human spirit. Successive government administrations continue to assume that there must be a moral flaw in those who do not instantly recognize the rightness and piety of our intentions. To our credit, Unitarian Universalists have been sufficiently sensitive to identify this tendency as religious idolatry. We are not alone in this, but we, along with others, do speak out candidly against the shameful practice of conscripting God as a tribal deity who smiles upon whatever any particular president decides is in "our national security interest," a God who is "on our side," a God itching to discomfit "godless communism." We are keen enough to sense that a religiosity that is merely an accessory of national purpose is a religiosity the Soviet leadership could tolerate as well.

There is little mystery about the spiritual need of an emerging world community. Albert Einstein once said that nuclear weapons had changed everything except the way humans think. Our profoundest spiritual need is for a new understanding of what it means to be human in a world that the human mind has succeeded in placing at ultimate risk. It must be an understanding illusionless enough to respect our limitations within a universe incomparably greater than ourselves and to reevaluate our potential for fashioning a sane, compassionate, and productive life within that frame. It must also be an understanding frank enough to accept ourselves as part of a naturalistic order, creatures who emerged from primordial earth, subject to destructive impulses that can be elaborated by the intricate cunning of a remarkable brain, but also creatures with transforming capabilities of thought, imagination, self-awareness, and caring cooperation. Further, it must be an understanding courageous enough to assert that humans are part of a moral order that knows no boundaries of sect or creed, outside of which we lose our meaning, but within which true redemption and transformation may be found.

Arnold Toynbee was Christian to the core, in belief and in practice. But his was also one of the new minds the world needs, and he spoke for Unitarian Universalists when he wrote:

> In the world in which we now find ourselves, the adherents of the different living religions ought to be readier to tolerate, respect, and revere one another's religious heritages because, in our generation, there is not anyone alive who is effectively in a position to judge between his own religion and his neighbor's. . . . If we do not feel that . . . we are confessing to a lack of faith in the truth and value of the religion that happens to be ours. On the other hand, if we do have faith in it, we shall have no fear that it will fail to play its full part in helping human souls to enter into communion with the presence behind the phenomena and to bring themselves into harmony with this Absolute Reality. The missions of the higher religions are not competitive; they are complementary. We can believe in our own religion without having to feel that it is the sole means of salvation (*A Historian's Approach to Religion*).

Those of us who dream of an onrushing day when all will become even as we are, need to take Toynbee to heart. He is talking to us as well as to others. For ourselves, we must have a view of life that sustains us and prepares us for living in the thorny world community of which we are a part. But we must not assume that we can immediately communicate our religious viewpoint to our world neighbors in convincing particulars. After all, we are not notably successful in communicating it to neighbors here at home. We must, in fact, strip ourselves of the irrelevant belief that for their own good all should accept our definition of what is rational. We must divest ourselves of the basically smug assumption that human progress and felicity are possible only in terms of our realities.

Liberal religion is something that can and does contribute to our becoming more serviceable participants in an emerging world community, as David Rankin enumerates in his eloquent essay "Defining Our Faith" on Unitarian Universalist beliefs:

> Like the Roman Catholics, we have a long tradition—extending back to the sun-baked desert of ancient Israel, the small rural villages of Transylvania, and the rocky shores of early New England.
>
> Like the Jews, we have our heroes and heroines—Servetus, David, and Fuller; Murray, Channing, and Emerson; Barton, Anthony, and Steinmetz—to name only a few.
>
> Like the Baptists, we have a system of democratic polity—with the congregation as the ultimate authority, an elected Board of Trustees, and a pulpit characterized by freedom of expression.
>
> Like the Confucianists, we have emphasized the capacity for reason—possessing a thirst for the fruits of wisdom and knowledge, and a reverent feeling toward the achievements of the mind.
>
> Like the Hindus, we have an eclectic system of theology—encouraging each individual to develop a personal faith which is not dependent on external demand.
>
> Like the Humanists, we have our roots in the experience

of the world—as it is known through the medium of touch, and sight, and sound, and taste, and smell.

Like the Buddhists, we have an accent on the individual—on the beauty, the mystery, and the holiness of each man, woman and child—as each is a sacred vessel.

The liberal spirit in religion, as we Unitarian Universalists know it, grew out of the Judeo-Christian tradition and is part of that tradition. But for most of us, it has grown to be more. Looking about us, we see that the liberal spirit has appeared in greater or lesser degree in all of the great faiths. It emerged in Hinduism in Buddha's teachings, then later as the Brahma Samaj. It appeared in cultic Judaism as the ethical thundering of the early prophets, then again in the efforts of Jesus to purify the moral imperatives of his ancestral faith. It sprang to life among the great philosophers of ancient Greece. Its story is that of the bursting of the cocoons religions spin around themselves. All the world faiths, as we see them today, are mixtures of contradictory impulses: the thrust to the closed, the particular, the chosen and the thrust to the open, the universal, the all-embracing.

Invariably, the narrowing instinct of each religion is deeply rooted in its past, beneath a hard crust of "exclusive" revelation. The devotees of God's incarnation in Christ must contend with the devotees of Allah's whisperings directly into the ear of Mohammed. But every faith also has its universalizing proclivity, one that is basically spiritual rather than mythical, ethical rather than doctrinal, social rather than sectarian. It is in this realm that the great faiths are in harmony:

> *In Hinduism:* Systems of faith differ, but God is one.
>
> *In Buddhism:* The good person's purpose is to increase the mercy, charity, kindness, and piety of all humankind.
>
> *In Judaism:* Who gains wisdom: Those who are willing to receive instruction from all sources.
>
> *In Zoroastrianism:* Diversity of worship has divided the human race into many creeds. From among all their dogmas

I have selected one—divine love.

In Shintoism: Regard heaven as your father, earth as your mother, and all things as your brothers and sisters.

In Confucianism: Love cannot be outnumbered.

In Christianity: Let us therefore follow after the things that make for peace and the things wherewith we may edify one another.

There is a distinctive note in each of the great religions. They cannot be better described than as the many strings of the harp. Their harmony flows from dealing with the same materials: human nature, human dependence on the transcendent, and human interdependence. Their highest aspirations are universal.

The religious liberalism of the Western world arose as the universalizing impulse within Judeo-Christianity and has grown gradually in its awareness of kinship with the same impulse in other great faiths. This is what led Emerson to study Asian religions and to their lasting imprint on his life and thought. This is what drew from his lips the passage in his Harvard Divinity School Address of July 15, 1838, that scandalized so many of his Unitarian peers: "Attach thyself not to the Christian symbol, but to the moral sentiment which carries innumerable Christianities, humanities and divinities in its bosom."

Channing, despite his staunch attachment to the Christian symbol, was moved to write: "Virtue is no local thing. It is not honorable because born in this community or that, but for its own, independent, lasting beauty." And he defined the bond of "the universal church" as one from which none could be "excommunicated" except by themselves, by "the death of goodness" in their own hearts.

In 1936, a newly established Commission on Appraisal of the American Unitarian Association issued a landmark report:

> What is needed is an association of free churches that will stand and fight for the central philosophy and values of liberal religion. . . . These churches . . . will be thoroughly

emancipated from the sectarian spirit, from the tendency to set themselves up as small, select, superior groups of men and women to whom by some mysterious dispensation an exclusive gift of truth has been granted. They will cultivate an intensive sense of fellowship within their own ranks, but they will be keenly aware of the world-wide aspects of their liberal faith, recognizing the kinship of liberals across all barriers of race, nationality or traditional religious background.

No document has ever been more prophetic. It recognized and gave impetus to an unmistakable trend. It reads today like a spiritual blueprint for a Unitarianism Universalism of the 1980s, witnessing the oneness of the universe, the oneness of the human family, the oneness of discovered and discoverable truth, the universal validity of free inquiry, and the dawn of universal humanity. We are not anti-Christian any more than we are anti-Moslem or anti-Buddhist. In fact, we are not anti anything except ignorance, dogmatism, bigotry, poverty, injustice, war, tyranny, and hypocrisy.

Our liberal faith is far from fully stretched to meet the spiritual needs of a new age. But we are beckoned to transform our faith into an adequate working force whose energies will not rest nor cease to mature as long as brotherhood/sisterhood, justice, and peace are the poorly realized dreams rather than the realities of our common life. In a time as dangerous to the human future as ours, the character of our liberal religious movement dare not stop short of the universal claims upon it.

The Who, What and Where of God

Go not, my soul, in search of him; thou wilt not find
   him there—
Or in the depths of shadow dim, or heights of upper air.
For not in far-off realms of space the Spirit hath its
   throne;
In ev'ry heart it findeth place and waiteth to
   be known.

FREDERICK LUCIAN HOSMER

All mother goddesses spin and weave. . . . Everything
that is comes out of them: They weave the world tapestry
out of genesis and demise, "threads appearing and disap-
pearing rhythmically."

HELEN DINER

Rich indeed have been our discoveries "in far-off realms of space."
Our spaceships and satellites, marvels of human technology, have
girdled the earth, landed on the moon, and orbited planets. Yet
none aboard them, or guiding them, would take issue with
Hosmer. There are no sightings out there of heaven's location or
God's throne. What is out there, our computer-directed invasions
confirm, is perhaps the most significant scientific discovery of our

age—infinite geometric space, within which, for practical human purposes, God is silent.

God does not speak in rational science's space. And it was Pascal, prescient and deeply Christian, who foresaw it when he wrote: "The eternal silences of the infinite frighten me."

From Pascal to the latest mind-boggling refinement in computer circuitry miniaturization, the impact on liberal religion is profound. The achievements of the scientific method inspire reverence in the minds of religious liberals. But there is confusion and sadness in their hearts. Science as science renounces all moral norms save the search for what is truly true and really real. Where, then, do we anchor all of the other moral issues and meanings of life? In a well-known anecdote, Napoleon asked a scientist where God figured in his model of the heavens. "Sir," the scientist answered, "I have no need of that hypothesis in my work." No need of that hypothesis in our scientific work perhaps. But what of the rest of life? Is there no need in that for all that is meant by "God's love of us" and "our love of God"? As Hosmer put it, "not in far-off realms of space . . . ," but what of "In ev'ry heart it findeth place and waiteth to be known"?

On yet another "God" front—feminist theology—religious liberals have responded, not with confusion and sadness, but with passionate enthusiasm. If in infinite geometric space there is no heavenly throne from which God roars "I am the Lord, thy God," isn't it equally bizarre to picture God as of one—or of any—gender? In part, God's maleness results from simple anthropomorphism, but it is also a product of the specifically Judeo-Christian conception of God, which was, and is, patriarchal. As feminist theologians like Rosemary Radford Ruether and Mary Daly have abundantly demonstrated, there was another early vision of deity within Judeo-Christianity, widespread until fiercely suppressed, which worshipped either a female goddess or a female aspect of divinity. Feminist theology's use of women's experience has been a critical force in liberal religion, along with science, in compelling a searching reexamination of the who, what, and where of God.

God as Problem

Male terminology has so permeated discussions of God as problem, that it is practically impossible to write much of what follows without using masculine characterizations.

Even to suggest that God might be a problem remains for many, despite science and feminist theology, a scandal and a blasphemy. Not so among Unitarian Universalists. God is a problem for several reasons, first because *God* is a word used to cover a multiplicity of meanings. Popularly, the word is used as if everyone understood the same things by it; but how can anyone, with reasonable consideration, claim that Albert Einstein's *God* is the same as Jerry Falwell's, or Rosemary Ruether's the same as Phyllis Schlafly's? This is one of the problems of God: a problem of language, of semantics, of perceptions. As my colleague Wallace Robbins once said: "Don't slap God on the back; you'll miss."

Another reason God is a problem grows out of what people sometimes know, but mostly do not know, about the historical evolution of God concepts. The God of a Hindu priest is a quite different product of spiritual development from the God of a Roman Catholic priest. Through the ages, the various divinities experienced and imagined by the human race have been of infinite and splendid variety. It is a great pity that they are not better known. A deeper appreciation of their richly diverse functions and natures might temper many of the hostilities among peoples of differing beliefs. Humanity's gods can only be known by those who take the trouble to investigate origins and comparative histories, and since so few bother, God *is* a problem of divisive misunderstandings and bitterness.

Still another problem is the symbolism of God. Religion deals with great, sweeping issues of destiny. When you ask someone how to get to the nearest post office, you anticipate a simple, direct answer. But when you ask someone sitting next to you on a plane, Where are we all going? you do not expect to be told Peoria. Religion strives for an overall account of the sum of things. It has an interest in totality, and God is the symbol most commonly used to express this cosmic perspective. But it is a tremendously large and encompassing symbol. Within its misty infinities, it is easy to become confused. Confused people lose their patience with one another. They find themselves contending for concrete definitions, and in the name of such definitions, massive slaughters have taken place.

Reasonable, temperate people come along who say that such strife is senseless. There is no way to prove *anything* about God, so why squander precious energies trying? Isn't it better simply to put the problem aside until we have more to go on? Meanwhile we can turn our attention to matters that yield to our current skills and knowledge. For the present, at least, the proper study for humans is humans. Let religion throw its entire and undistracted force into the struggle to extricate the human enterprise from its present dire failings and dilemmas. Someday we may know enough to make responsible statements about God. At present this is not possible.

I have described here the view of a significant company of sincerely religious persons both within and outside the Unitarian Universalist body. Yet many are not so willing to suspend their quest for God. Asking ultimate questions may be impractical, but one of reason's compulsions is asking.

We recognize from the start that it is undesirable to press for conformity of profession about the nature of God. As I have suggested, for some it seems better to leave the symbol God in abeyance until there is more to go on. For others, it is a symbol representing, however intangibly, the precious quest for deeper and deeper meanings. None of us tries to compel others to believe one thing or another about God, but every Unitarian Universalist assumes an obligation to know as fully as possible the facets of human experience out of which theologies arise.

The human race has told itself many stories about human origins, destinies, and relationships with forces called gods and God. These stories have two common elements: They reflect the ordinary anxieties and strivings of daily life, and they recognize the existence of forces humans may never actually see or touch, but which must be taken into account in describing the realities of birth-to-death human living. Inevitably these stories raise puzzling questions. Are humans but meaningless specks in infinite wastes of space and time, helpless victims of random forces, careless products of invisible energies, creatures like the fisherman in Hemingway's *The Old Man and the Sea* who catches the largest fish of his scrabbly career only to have it devoured by sharks before he can bring it to shore? Are good and evil as casual, as coincidental, as impersonal as the catch and the shark? Are humans, as Lewis Mumford posed it, "a smoking candle with a charred wick . . . a poor flame flickering in a wind that will speedily extinguish it"?

Or are humans the epicenter of divine attention, the wayward children of a majestic deity, creatures who have flaunted their rebellious will in the face of a Father-God and placed their souls in eternal jeopardy? Have they, by their disobedience, thrust themselves out of a Garden of Eden where they were at one with all creation? Is their nature both earthly and divine, but so steeped in the sins of assertiveness and pride that it cannot overcome damnation except through the gift of divine grace? Is it true that humans can find the answers they seek only if they prepare themselves, by the right beliefs, for another world and turn all their hopes and energies toward it?

This is the story orthodox Christianity tells to the world, and with certain variations (some of them important), it is a story told by many religions. Actually, the notion that earthly life is a vale of human sin from which there is rescue only by divine fiat is far older than Christianity.

How do people think their way through such dilemmas as the traditional myths pose? They do so, quite naturally, within their own limits. Since their own earthly lives have a beginning and an end, they think of the universe in the same way. It, too, must begin and end. Humans understand best the things they themselves have a hand in creating. In an effort to understand the universe, they assume that there must be a creator who stands outside creation and controls it. Early metaphysical thinking was done at a time when kings or their equivalent ruled with despotic authority over property, behavior, ideas, and even life. Representative democracy and the consent of the governed were far in the future. Consequently, people thought about the most powerful gods, or God, as both male and almighty.

It is difficult for most Unitarian Universalists to understand why people have continued through the ages to fashion God in this image. Even more to the point, since Pascal anyway, is the question of God as creator. If God is creator, was he himself uncreated? John Stuart Mill, in his autobiography, wrote:

> My father taught me that the question "Who made me?" cannot be answered, since it immediately suggests the further question "Who made God?" Here in this very simple sentence is the enormous fallacy in all the so-called proofs of God's existence as a First Cause. If everything must have a cause, then God too must be caused. If there is anything without a cause, it might just as well be you as God.

Bertrand Russell ran one of his celebrated numbers on the Mill conundrum, pointing out that it is like the ancient Hindu view that the world is resting upon an elephant and the elephant upon a tortoise. When someone asks, "What about the tortoise?" the Hindu says, "Let's change the subject."

The argument for God as creator, as Kant and many others have pointed out, is unconvincing. Logic throws no obstacle to the notion that the universe has *always* existed. But the human imagination shrinks from this. The need to think in terms of beginnings and ends is strong, so humans speculate about God as creator and first cause, and lead themselves to the conviction that God, though in the midst of his creation, is separated from it by incalculable distance. God is in the midst of the human scene (immanent), indeed is within each one of us, yet dwarfs the whole of creation by his awesome power and perfection. Is it not fair to say that such a God, in terms of reason, is actually more of a problem than the problems his existence is presumed to solve?

Baffled by the very mysteries they create for themselves, humans, the ineffable theologians, plunge into further contradictions. On the one hand, God is pictured as pure spirit: nameless, fathomless, infinite; on the other hand, he incarnates himself as Krishna in Hinduism, as Buddha in (some forms of) Buddhism, as Christ in Christianity. The intention is admirable enough: It is to account in some way for the existence of a divine element in human life and to give to it an intimate reality. But for our lives to have the meaning and purpose we require of them, is it necessary for us to confound ourselves by setting forth these competing incarnations as material facts? Is it necessary to try to make an uncreated creator out of God—a cosmic, male satrap? Will we slide into moral nihilism unless we think of the cosmic process as a predetermined plan existing first in the mind of God and then unfolding itself like a giant edict before our eyes?

The persistent habit of traditional religions is to shape their demands upon communicants around a God who is responsible for everything that is and is to be. God, in the classic phraseology, is all-powerful, all-knowing, and omnipresent. In the Ninetieth Psalm's flowing description:

> Lord, thou hast been our dwelling place in all generations.
> Before the mountains were brought forth,
> Or ever thou hadst formed the earth and the world,
> Even from everlasting to everlasting, thou art God.

God, in other words, is at the beginning of all things and in a position of active, conscious responsibility for everything.

A Unitarian Universalist does not shrink from recognizing that such a God is a staggering dilemma. If God is put at the beginning, as the creator of all things, the power responsible for all things, he becomes a monstrous being. This, in truth, is what many sensitive spiritual souls, down through the centuries, have intuited. Any God who is responsible for everything is, at least in part, a god of violence, pain, misery, injustice, and cruelty. As a piece of folk wisdom has it: "If God is God, then God is not good; if God is good, then God is not God. Take the even; take the odd."

If you try to apologize for this God, who has presumably produced a creation at least half lost to the powers of evil, by saying
that he promises redemption for the elect, you merely turn a brutal
deity into a demented one. What would we think, for example, of a
human father who deliberately torments his children with debasement and terror, then turns around and lavishes favors on one of
them while leaving the others to tremble and whimper? As shock-
ing as such an act would be, it is less so than the behavior of an
Almighty who is capable of condemning human beings to an eternity of awful suffering for sins committed in the briefest of lifetimes
in a world for which this King of the Universe is avowedly responsible. Here is a savagely disproportionate system of punishment that
is an insult not only to reason but to justice as well.

Yet, children are being indoctrinated every day with such teachings. The daughter of one of my colleagues came home on the verge
of hysteria because a playmate told her that if she was bad God
would send her to burn forever in hell. She was reminded of the
mild disciplines she experienced at home, when they were ab-
solutely necessary, and was told that if Mommy and Daddy could be
that gentle when provoked, how much more gentle God must be.

It is a reasonably good answer to a child, yet it begs the question. If God is really at the beginning of things, if God truly controls, then it is small wonder that he could shock Voltaire with the
slaughter of innocents. We can imagine what Voltaire would say
about a God who permits his creatures to build crematories in
Buchenwald, to atom-bomb Hiroshima, to exterminate Afghan
villages, and to practice apartheid in South Africa.

Neither faith nor reason can refuse to face such questions. If
divine planning actually presides over all the occasions of human
life, then God, from a human point of view, is part demon. If God
is all-powerful, responsible for all that happens, capable of heed-
ing even the sparrow's fall, then he can hardly be a loving God. By
the same token, if God, from a human point of view, is truly a loving God, he cannot by any means be all-powerful. Indeed, it is precisely this that led in ancient times to divine dualisms, a God of

good locked in combat with a God of evil, and both contending for the control of human affairs. Zoroastrianism and early Manichean Christianity are examples. In our day, there is renewed interest in what used to be called a limited God: a God who is loving but not all-powerful, a God who struggles against primordial, untamed chaos and evil. Attesting to a widespread sympathetic response is the popularity of books, sermons, and church school curriculum units around the general theme of why bad things happen to good people. The difficulties of dealing with two supreme deities, or one limited God, are no less vexing to faith and reason than those associated with one God, omnipotent, omniscient, and omnipresent.

Questions such as these form some of our strongest bonds of liberal religious fellowship. We know that the issues are real, pertinent, and searching. We know that they cannot be dismissed with pulpit platitudes. We draw together in common revulsion before those who speak of God as some kind of cosmic Big Brother who will set everything right if we just put his name on enough coins, stamps, public buildings, and schoolroom walls.

Unitarian Universalists share a realization that if the traditional Almighty is real, he is beyond human comprehension and unworthy of human worship. We are inclined, in this instance, to agree with Julius Penrose in James Cozzen's novel *By Love Possessed* that theology is "the homage . . . nonsense pays to sense."

In what ways, then, do we characteristically look for solutions to the problem of God? There are three main lines of direction: God and the human search for self, God and idealized reality, God and the search for meaning and purpose.

May the Inner and the Outer Person Be One

What motivates people in their religious beliefs? The picture that emerges from research is hardly cause for unalloyed rejoicing. A project done for the American Anthropological Association reports the sad finding that intense religiousness springs more often from fear and anger than from love and peace. This would seem to confirm what psychotherapists have long noted when treating persons whose emotional distresses include a pronounced religious element. Mary McCarthy underscores this in a paragraph in *Memories of a Catholic Girlhood*: "From what I have seen, I am driven to the conclusion that religion is only good for good people, and I do not mean this as a paradox, but simply as an observable fact. Only good people can afford to be religious. For others, it is too great a temptation—a temptation to the deadly sins of pride and anger, chiefly, but one might also add sloth. My Grandmother McCarthy, I am sure, would have been a better woman if she had been an atheist or an agnostic."

Religious belief may all too easily become a weapon in the hands of infantile adults, justifying and sanctifying hostile and fear-ridden behavior. For many of us the search for God is a search for self. So far so good. But if we find God too easily and in too stereotyped a form, we are likely to end with a none-too-admirable self. God can be a vehicle for immaturity.

Until the beginning of our century, nearly all matters concerning the human psyche were referred to theologians and philosophers. In the late eighteenth century, for example, psychology was taught in the same departments at Harvard and Yale as angelology. Ancient Athens, with its deeper respect for psychological insights, turned to philosophers for guidance. Thus Socrates, in one of his infrequent prayers, gave this memorable prescription for spiritual health: "Beloved Pan, and all ye other gods that haunt this place, give me beauty in the inward soul, and may the inner and the outer . . . be at one."

Centuries later, Augustine, a person of many facets, developed a keen eye for psychological truths. He taught that persons find themselves only when they are able to penetrate deeply enough into their experience to unite the subjective and objective aspects of their lives. It is also at this point, Augustine said, that a person finds God.

If we continue up the slopes of history to the nineteenth century, before the advent of Sigmund Freud, we find the most penetrating psychological insights being offered by Kierkegaard and Nietzsche, both philosophers and both intensely interested in religion. Contrary to a widespread impression of his work, it was Nietzsche who sensed more clearly than most that without corresponding advances in human moral character, technical progress could lead to ethical nihilism. In reaction to this grave danger, he wrote his familiar dramatic parable of the madman who comes into a village asking, "Where is God?" The people laugh and answer that God has emigrated, gone on a trip. The madman then cries: "I will tell you where God has gone. We have killed him, you and I. We have unchained this earth from its sun. God remains dead, and we have killed him." At this point, the madman lapses into silence, gazing at the people. They, too, become silent, looking at him. Then he speaks his final words: "I come too early. This tremendous event is still on its way."

Nietzsche was issuing an indictment against a mechanization of life that crushes the self and the ethical sense. The "tremendous event . . . still on its way" was, as he accurately predicted, the onrushing fury of twentieth-century collectivism (George Orwell's *1984*), with its transformation of persons into automatons without heart or soul.

The developing science of psychology became itself a portion of the mechanistic tendency. Pavlov's conditioned-response experiments in the Soviet Union and B.F. Skinner's behaviorism in the United States cannot be called premeditated attempts to dehumanize humans. Far from it. Both had the underlying humanistic purpose of discovering better ways to release persons from the tyranny of fear and hostility. But from these and similar efforts an attempt continues to construct a total psychological view of human behavior based on mechanistic principles, disregarding such unquantifiable abstractions as mind and consciousness. This flaw is alarming to most religious liberals. Humans ought never to be just conditioned creatures, the complete captives of a chain of stimulus and response. Humans transcend conditioning. They exercise choice by virtue of their capacity for self-awareness. Their margins of choice are narrow—to this extent behavioral psychology is correct—but within such margins they find the meaning of freedom and responsibility. Here, also, is the dwelling place of their higher religious yearnings and their quest to understand the purposes of their being.

Most psychologists today are unwilling to be classified among the mechanistic thinkers. The tide in psychology, as among practitioners of the harder sciences, is toward a more open view. This is not to say that the wider scientific horizons offer proof, however fuzzy, of particular conceptions of God. But it is now scientifically respectable to examine what, for many, had been a closed area and to seek ideas of a ground of being that sustain and magnify the human sense of freedom and ethical responsibility.

The coming of Sigmund Freud, interestingly enough, helped to turn the search for God inward. Freud's work had a shattering effect on traditional understandings of faith and morals. He demonstrated that many of the real reasons for our behavior have little to do with conscious theological beliefs, but stem instead from wishes, fears, and experiences of which we have no conscious awareness. With Freud's findings as guides, it was possible to demonstrate that pious behavior is often motivated by repressed hate of self rather than by love of God. Freud hovers behind Mary McCarthy's pained observation that only people who are good to begin with should risk the temptation of becoming ardent religious believers.

The popularization of Freud's theories sent waves of alarm through the minds of many sincere ethical and religious thinkers. It seemed that a new type of determinism was being forced on the human species, this time in the guise of unconscious drives and instincts. Freud himself argued that the Judeo-Christian concept of God was an extension of infantile dependency.

Once again, however, the meanings suggested by Freud's pioneering work have been broadened by the trend away from a mechanistic interpretation of science. Psycholanalytic thinkers such as Jung, Adler, Horney, Fromm, and Kohut have built on Freud's discoveries and have used the fruits of his genius to encourage a deepened and more positive interest in the role of ethics and religion. It became possible to assert that ethics cannot be attained by being dishonest with oneself, and that the idea of God as a cosmic father who will always take care of his right-believing children is inadequate. Freud's historic accomplishment, broadened by those who came after him, puts a fresh gloss on Socrates's prayer. The oneness of the inner and the outer person, a unity of the self, is the basis for sound ethics and creative religious beliefs.

Liberal religion is not driven by a conflict between psychology and religion. To us, psychoanalysis and psychotherapy are not substitutes for religion, but are exciting, useful tools for helping to clear away some of the debris of anxiety, guilt, and hostility that keeps us from enlarging our precious margins of freedom. Our purpose is to arrive at ethical and religious beliefs that will be most expressive of the self and of the real situation in which we live. Augustine said that persons find God when they find self. There is nothing in modern psychology that should persuade anyone, in the name of science, to dispute Augustine's contention. A concept of God emerging from a unified, unblocked, fully functioning self bears its own spiritual warrant. To plumb the levels of the unconscious is to tap springs of insight, creativity, and energy beyond anything most people are conscious of possessing. For many of us, the discovery of self is indeed, as Augustine suggested, the beginning of a discovery of an experience of God.

If self-discovery results in greater self-affirmation, what happens to the traditional idea of dependence on God? This is a serious issue, if for no other reason than that it divides people into conflicting camps. From the evangelical side come the common, comforting affirmations: "What a friend we have in Jesus" and "God will take care of you." From the brasher advocates of psychological scientism we hear warnings to depend on no one or nothing but one's self or suffer the consequences of immaturity and crippled self-regard.

It is wise to rephrase the problem. How can we, on one hand, resolve to be accountable to ourselves and to others for our own actions, develop and use our own powers, and mind that each person take responsibility in the long run for the development of her or his own life and, on the other hand, acknowledge that we exist in a world of "givens" that are much weightier than we are no matter how faithfully we apply ourselves to high moral tasks?

When the question is asked in this manner, we can reasonably hope to demonstrate that truly creative people are those who affirm themselves and their talents to the fullest extent but at the same time acknowledge their dependence both on life's unmerited favors, forces, and circumstances and on their need for others. We might call this a Unitarian Universalist's tripartite principle of self-assertion, grace, and community. We all have resources of creativity for which we are starkly and relentlessly responsible. At the same time, we live in circumstances over which we exercise little or no control. And we are in this condition together. How we are to adjust ourselves to this reality is each person's basic religious challenge. Ours is not the effrontery of rejecting the solution of those who *do* accept the "revealed" answers of traditional theology and find by doing so that they are able to keep growing, make fuller use of their powers, and deepen their humility and capacity for awe, wonder, and service. But for us, Freud was right in saying that the idea of God can be used for anything but constructive ethical and religious purposes. By the same token, we also discipline ourselves to remember that a superficial skepticism, untempered by an abiding sense of the mysteries of which we are a part, *can* be an unwholesome spiritual arrogance.

Fortunately, there is a healthy kind of pride in one's own powers that goes hand in hand with humility, and it delineates liberal religion at its best. For lack of a better term, we call it self-esteem: a willingness to assert, without guilt, our capacities for freedom, responsibility, creativity, and community, while affirming, without anxiety, our constant dependence on forces beyond ourselves. Never need we fear to assert ourselves as long as we are able to feel a proportionate awe in realizing that truth is always greater than our grasp of it. Indeed, the truth we do *not* know grows larger precisely as we discover more truth. We are free to rejoice in the use of our talents, to exult in our abilities to feel, create, and grow, in proportion to our wonder at the vast mystery of grace that surrounds us. To esteem ourselves properly means that we esteem also the people about us and the indescribable, immeasurable reality of which we are all part. For many of us, God is this reality. Self-assertion and dependence are reconciled. The religious person and the spiritually healthy person become one.

To Find the Province of the Divine

Let me return for a moment to James Cozzen's novel *By Love Possessed*. Arthur Winner, Jr., the central figure, is musing about the religious views of his father:

> In short, did the Man of Reason ever accept the story of the incarnate godhead, or the story of the risen Christ . . . ? The Man of Reason had done the reading of his day and what was he being told (by his friend, the rector) but the very stuff of myth—the woman got with child by the deity in time to bear the infant savior at the winter solstice; the grievous formal murder of the theanthropos whose earth-breaking return from the dead must occur near the vernal equinox. Could the Man of Reason credit the dreadful drama's orthodox accounting-for? Could ethical assent ever be given by him to all the shocking, the really monstrous, dogma of the atonement implied? What was here but allegorical fantasy, a laborious attempt in symbols to relate the finite known to the infinite unknown? You received such stories, not as shedding light on, but as admitting, the mystery awesome and permanent of life.

Those who have borne with my self-revelations in this book so far will instantly recognize why these lines touch and delight me. I arrived long ago where Arthur Winner, Sr., arrived, with a sureness of feeling that the God whose substance can be verified only by such tortuous dogmas as the atonement is a God who sheds no light on the awesome and permanent mysteries of life. Then what does a person do? If that person is Arthur Winner, Sr., he remains in the Episcopal Church, telling himself that the stuff of myth has long been the sacred fiction of his family and of his class, a fable so honored that it has a vested right.

Another option is one claimed by me and my chosen coreligionists, who seek the province of the divine in precincts other than those established for the veneration of ancient myths and creeds. We look for sustaining and satisfying intimations of God within the vested right of the free mind.

Such a coreligionist, for example, was Baruch Spinoza, master mathematician and philosopher of the seventeenth century's liberal Dutch Republic. In 1656, Spinoza was excommunicated from the Jewish community of Amsterdam for "abominable heresies." His crime was seeking an experience of God acceptable to people of reason, independent thought, and ethical sensitivity—not a God of revelation, but a God of nature.

Spinoza began with nature and divided it into two parts. One part is the active, invisible, vital process of nature: its creative force; the other is the massive product of creative force: the tangible, individual items, modes, or forms such as trees, winds, waters, hills, fields, stones, flowers, mountains, animals, and human beings. For Spinoza, God *as substance* is the first part of nature and God *as extension* is the second. God is the vital, creative process and force beneath and within all things. God is the universe and all that is in it.

Spinoza then asked what we mean when we speak of the help of God. He answered that the help of God means the fixed and unchangeable order of nature, or the chain of natural events. The universal laws of nature and the decrees of God are one and the same. To use Spinoza's words: "From the infinite nature of God, all things follow by the same necessity, and in the same way, as it follows from the nature of a triangle, from eternity to eternity, that its three angles are equal to two right angles" (*Treatise on God and Man*).

What the laws of the triangle are to all triangles, God is to the world. Therefore, since the will of God and the laws of nature are one and the same, it follows that all events in human life, and outside it, are governed by dependable, invariable laws, and not by the whim of an autocrat seated in the heavens. Spinoza concluded that our gravest human error is to try to make God a conscious creature like ourselves, with changeable desires and purposes. Our problem of evil, in which we attempt to reconcile the ills of life with the presumed goodness of God, is a purely human problem having nothing to do with God. Spinoza chided those who forgot the lesson of Job that God is beyond our human problems of good and evil. Good and evil are relative to human tastes and experiences. They have no meaning in the universe as a whole.

As to the question of whether God is in any sense a person, Spinoza answers no. If triangles could speak, they would describe God as triangular. If circles could speak, they would describe God as circular. If horses could speak, they would describe God as horselike. It is natural but incorrect for humans to ascribe their own attributes to God.

The will of God, Spinoza continues, is the sum of all causes and all laws. The intellect of God is the sum of all mind. The mental and molecular processes that constitute the double reality of the universe—their causes and their laws—are God. Because this is a lawful universe, we must apply a measured understanding to human actions. As reason provides us with the perception of God behind the flux of things in the universe, so reason enables us to discover law in the flux of human desires and purposes. The action of reason is human liberty, and it is the only real freedom available to us. We are free to the extent that we know and understand ourselves, our fellows, and the world in which we live. Thus do we fortify ourselves to bear both faces of fortune. God is not a capricious personality, absorbed in the private affairs of worshippers, but the invariable, sustaining order of the universe. Moral persons, perceiving things through this eye of eternity, rise above fitful yearnings to identify their personal pleasures and desires with God and achieve a high serenity of contemplation and ethical wisdom.

Little wonder that Spinoza is the prototype of many present-day Unitarian Universalists. His was a lasting, impressive monument of brave faith in a magnificently credible and impersonal God. The province of the divine discovered by this inspired grinder of lenses plays a vital role still in the making of liberal religious minds.

James Luther Adams, the foremost theologian and ethicist of contemporary Unitarian Universalism, grapples directly with what is meant by "the love of God." He describes it as "the giving of oneself to the power that holds the world together and that, when we are tearing it apart, persuades us to come to ourselves and start on new beginnings" (*The Love of God*). Why is this kind of love reliable? Because it alone "has within it the seeds of becoming, even in the face of tragedy and death—when it keeps confidence, saying, 'Into thy hands I commend my spirit.'" What is also reliable about this kind of love is the special respect it engenders for the necessary diversity of human beings. Because this love is a giving over of self to a process of transformation, all persons who experience it in their relations to each other and in their diversity "become mutually supporting and enhancing rather than mutually impoverishing."

The seemingly intractable antagonism between egoism and altruism is "transcended in the devotion to the good of others, which is at the same time the fulfillment of the good of the self." As Adams expresses it:

> In the fellowship of the love of God one loses life to find it. And yet the loss and the finding are more than the process of self-realization. We become new creatures. This is the work of God that brings the self to something more than and beyond the self, beyond even the "highest self."

Adams warns that no rosy path is promised by this kind of love.

> It may lead to what Thomas à Kempis calls "the royal way of the cross," a way which God as well as man traverses, not for the sake of suffering in itself to be sure, but for the sake of suffering, separated humankind. A comprehending mutuality

rooted in immemorial being stirs . . . itself anew to heal and unite what has been wounded and separated.

Adams reasons that the love of God is a love we can give only because it was first given to us.

Ultimately, it is not even ours to give, for it is not in our keeping. It is in the keeping of a power that we can never fully know, of a power that we must in faith trust. Humanity's expression of it is a response to an antecedent glory and promise, the ground of meaning and the ever new resource for its fulfillment.

Is there a test we can apply? Indeed there is, says Adams. "By their fruits shall ye know them." To learn what is meant by professed love of God, watch "what sort of behavior issues from it." The best way to demonstrate the power of a religious-ethical profession is "to show what difference it makes in action." In fact, we commonly apply this test in personal behavior terms, noting that love of God that is deficient in "individual integrity, in humility, and in affectionate concern for others, is counterfeit."

But Adams is not content to let the matter rest in personal attitudes and behavior alone. He insists that love of God is clearly and relevantly manifest only "when we know what it means for institutional behavior, when we know what kind of family, or economic system, or political order it demands." As an example of decisive difference, he compares and contrasts the family patterns of "the old Lutherans and the Quakers." Their words about the love of God are, on the surface, much the same. "The one group," however, "sanctioned a sort of patriarchal family in which the authoritarian father was the vicar of God in the home, and love of God among the children was supposed to produce instant, unquestioning obedience; the other group preferred a family in which a more permissive, persuasive atmosphere prevailed. Yet both groups avowed the love of God as proclaimed in the Gospels." Adams concludes that the true meanings of professed religious imperatives become concrete only when seen in a social context: "Often the meaning of an ethical generality can be determined by observing what its proponents wish to change in society or to preserve unchanged."

The profound impact that James Luther Adams had on the theological quest of Unitarian Universalists is perhaps best summarized in his words:

> Those who interpret the love of God as movement toward a community of freedom and mutuality will be able to vindicate the claim that they serve a power that is reliable, only by yielding to that power in the midst of a world that is suffering, divided by cleavages of race, class, and nation. What is at stake is the creation of a world in which this kind of love of God becomes incarnate in a more just and free society.

Rosemary Radford Ruether, a feminist Christian theologian, has no organic bond with Unitarian Universalism, but her nonsexist understandings of God are a bracing tonic for many within our ranks. With bold strokes, she challenges ages-old interpretations of religious experience that are rooted in a male elitist perspective. Women, she writes, have been systematically subordinated and negated in a system of language about God, "man," nature, sin, and redemption that is male-centered. With unassailable scholarly credentials, she mines the teachings of the Bible and the writings of ancient Goddess-oriented cultures, concluding that the patriarchal bias in religion was not always so nor need it be today. Widening her embrace to include the liberation theologies of all oppressed peoples, she points the way to a fuller vision of God/ess, one that undergirds a positive, egalitarian faith.

To fill in the picture, I will let Ruether speak for herself in an imaginary interview, with all of her answers drawn from her book *Sexism and God-Talk.*

JM: How would you describe the critical principle of feminist theology?

RRR: "[It] is the promotion of the full humanity of women.

Whatever denies, diminishes, or distorts the full humanity of women is, therefore, appraised as not redemptive, [and] must be presumed not to reflect the divine or an authentic relation to the divine, . . . or a community of redemption."

JM: Can you phrase this in more positive terms?

RRR: "[Gladly.] What does promote the full humanity of women is the Holy, it does reflect true relation to the divine, it is the true nature of things, the authentic message of redemption and the mission of redemptive community. But the meaning of this positive principle—namely, the full humanity of women—is not fully known. What we have known is . . . the denigration and marginalization of women's humanity. Still, the humanity of women . . . has not been destroyed. It has constantly affirmed itself, often in only limited and subversive ways, and it has been the touchstone against which we test and criticize all that diminishes us. In the process we experience our larger potential that allows us to begin to imagine a world without sexism. . . . The uniqueness of feminist theology is not the critical principle, full humanity, but the fact that women claim this principle for themselves. Women name themselves [as *imago dei*, in the image of God] as subjects of authentic and full humanity."

JM: Would you explain again how you think sexism has corrupted this principle?

RRR: "[By] the naming of males as norms of authentic humanity. . . . This distorts and contradicts the theological paradigm of *imago dei*/Christ. Defined as male humanity against or above women, as ruling-class humanity above servant classes, the *imago dei*/Christ paradigm becomes an instrument of sin rather than a disclosure of the divine and an instrument of grace."

JM: Doesn't this imply that "women cannot simply reverse the sin of sexism[;] cannot simply scapegoat males for historical evil in a way that makes themselves only innocent victims"?

RRR: "Women cannot [and must not] affirm themselves as *imago dei* and subjects of full human potential in a way that diminishes male humanity. Women, as the denigrated half of the human species, must reach for a continually expanding definition of inclusive humanity—inclusive of both genders, inclusive of all social groups and races. Any principle of religion or society that marginalizes one group of persons as less than fully human diminishes us all. In rejecting androcentrism (males as norms of humanity), women must also criticize all other forms of chauvinism: making white Westerners the norm of humanity, making Christians the norm of humanity, making privileged classes the norm of humanity. Women must also criticize humanocentrism, that is, making humans the norm and crown of creation in a way that diminishes the other beings in the community of creation."

JM: But isn't there a danger here of leveling everything into a deadening kind of sameness?

RRR: "This is not a question of sameness but of recognition of value, which at the same time affirms genuine variety and particularity. It reaches for a new mode of relationship, neither a hierarchical model that diminishes the potential of the 'other' nor an 'equality' defined by a ruling norm drawn from the dominant group; rather a mutuality that allows us to affirm different ways of being."

JM: One last question. It is about your use of the term God/ess. What do you mean by it?

RRR: "If all human language for God/ess is analogy, if taking a particular human image literally is idolatry, then male language for the divine must lose its privileged place. . . . Images of God/ess must include female roles and experiences. Images of God/ess must be drawn from the activities of peasants and working people, people at the bottom of society. Most of all, images of God/ess must be transformative, pointing us back to our authentic potential and forward to new redeemed possibilities. . . . Feminist theology needs to affirm the God of Exodus, of liberation and new being, but as rooted in . . . God/ess as Matrix, as source and ground of our being [and] . . . of our being-new [who] does not lead us back to a stifled, dependent self or uproot us in a spirit-trip outside the earth. . . . The liberating encounter with God/ess is always an encounter with our authentic selves resurrected from underneath the alienated self. It is not experienced against, but in and through relationships, healing our broken relations with our bodies, with other people, with nature. We have no adequate name for the true God/ess, the 'I am who I shall become.' Intimations of Her/His name will appear as we emerge from false naming of God/ess modeled on patriarchal alienation."

Through the use of unique, individual expressions such as we find in Spinoza, Adams, and Ruether, I have attempted to sketch some of the God and God/ess concepts available to and influencing the theologies of various Unitarian Universalists. Once again it is important to stress the range of diversity not only permitted but encouraged in our free fellowship of religious seekers and affirmers. For us, faith is forever struggling to come into existence. It is a design still fully to emerge, a rationality still to be achieved, a justice still to be established, a love still to be fulfilled.

Whatever Yields to Human Guidance

Finally, we turn our attention to still another faith stance, one that exercises great influence not only among us, but also among concerned and thoughtful people the world around. It is religious humanism, an ethically based spiritual position that abjures theological supernaturalism and metaphysical dualism even as it resists and rejects all-out secularism.

According to Francis Bacon, we humans are empowered not only to live more creatively within the natural world but also to shape more creatively a moral world. We can accept responsibility for bettering the ethical environment, taking firmer command of our lives, finding new ways of seeing old facts and patterns, going beneath appearances to deeper levels of meaning and purpose. Bacon believed, far ahead of his time, that there is no better way to become fully human than to give birth to a conscious faith that is one's own. He was a post-Reformation herald of what we now know as religious humanism, which may or may not be, as an English bishop has said, the religion of "fifty percent of the intelligent people of the modern world," but is, by all recent surveys, the religion of a plurality of contemporary Unitarian Universalists.

Religious humanism has ancient foundations. A millennium before the birth of Jesus, the Aeolians, Dorians, and Ionians swept into Greece from the north, bringing their gods with them. For centuries, the wisest among them wrestled with the task of accommodating these gods to a new land and a new way of life. Their speculations became steadily more obscure. Finally, some 450 years before the Christian era, a voice spoke out in ringing protest against the unintelligible popular theology. It was Protagoras's voice: "As for the Gods, I do not know whether they exist or not. Life is too short for such difficult enquiries. . . . Humans are the measure of all things."

For his outburst of frustration, Protagoras was exiled. Seeking haven in Sicily, he was lost at sea. Inquisitors poked into the corners and closets of his homeland, ferreting every copy of his books they could find and burning them in the public square. Nevertheless, Protagoras is justly remembered as the pioneer humanist. His is still the classical definition of humanism—an approach to faith, thought, and action that assigns an overriding interest to the human rather than to the supernatural.

In current terms, people look at the enormous religious energies expended on scanning, worshipping, supplicating, and propitiating a God who may or may not exist, and, like Protagoras, they say:

Wait a minute! I don't want any part of this. Life is too short and too endangered. Let's change the focus to what we know exists—human beings and their demonstrated capabilities for good and evil. Let's concentrate our moral passions on what we can do about that!

Bertrand Russell said his humanist faith sprung ultimately from an admiration of two human qualities: kindly feeling and veracity. Speaking of kindly feeling, he wrote:

> Most of the social and political evils of the world arise through absence of sympathy and presence of hatred, envy, or fear. . . . Every kind of hostile action or feeling provokes a reaction by which it is increased and so generates a progeny of violence and injustice which has a terrible vitality. This can only be met by cultivating in ourselves and attempting to generate in the young feelings of friendliness rather than hostility, of well-wishing rather than malevolence, and of cooperation rather than competition (*Lecture on Humanism*).

Russell said that when he is asked why he believes this, he does not appeal to any supernatural authority, but only to the common human wish for happiness:

> A world full of hate is a world full of sorrow. . . . From the point of view of worldly wisdom, hostile feeling and limitation of sympathy are folly. Their fruits are war, death, oppression, and torture, not only for their original victims but, in the long run, also for their perpetrators or their descendants.

The opposite is also true, Russell said. If we could all learn to love our neighbors, the world would very rapidly become a better place for us all. This is why he regards veracity as second only to kindly feeling. The key to veracity is believing according to evidence and not because a belief is comfortable or a source of power, pride, or pleasure. Self-deception—the absence of veracity—is the classic enemy of love of truth. In Russell's words:

It is very easy for those who have exceptional power to persuade themselves that the system by which they profit gives more happiness to underdogs than they would enjoy under a more just system. And, even where no obvious bias is involved, it is only by means of veracity that we can acquire the scientific knowledge required to bring about our common purposes.

Russell asks that we reflect on how many cherished prejudices had to be abandoned in the development of modern medicine and hygiene, and how many wars would have been prevented by a just estimate of the prospects rather than one based on conceit and wishful thinking. He proposes that we apply these considerations especially to religious beliefs. Unproven and unprovable "revelations" are not really needed to help us see that human welfare requires a less ferocious ethic. More and more people are unable to accept traditional beliefs anyway. To think that apart from these beliefs there is no foundation for kindly behavior is to invite disaster. That is why, Russell concludes, "it is important to show that no supernatural reasons are needed to make humans kind and to prove that only through kindness can the human race achieve happiness."

As we turn to a crisp summary of humanism's major affirmations, let me first distinguish the movement in religious thought from the school in general culture that also calls itself humanism, and whose most celebrated advocates of the recent past include Irving Babbitt and Paul Elmer More. The link between the two is that both are fundamentally concerned with the human condition, and especially with the distinctive values that humans are capable of realizing. Beyond this link, however, there are marked differences, greatest perhaps in religious matters. Babbitt had little sympathy for religious interests. More, on the other hand, championed Anglo-Catholicism, a position far from religious humanism.

The primary professions of religious humanism are these:

Concerning the human moral situation. Any honest reading of history reveals that moral values are relative to changing human experience. The shareable social values, however, maintain and enhance their excellence in the face of all doubt and criticism.

Humans need not only the satisfaction of particular wants but also the attainment of integrated personalities. This result is best achieved by earnest devotion to the shareable social goods. Such devotion is the essence of religion.

Concerning metaphysics. Scientific method is the most dependable guide to truth about the world. The universe is an objective order, which takes no account of human good or evil except so far as humans control parts of it toward their own ends.

There are no guarantees of good's ultimate victory, nor of the eternal preservation of human values. Intelligent devotion to the highest values does not require such guarantees. The ultimate faith in religion is faith in the worthwhileness of human good.

Concerning social ethics. The most important values that maintain their excellence in the face of all doubt and criticism are scientific truth (veracity), moral and artistic creativity, and love (kindness and justice). The joy of comradeship (community) in the quest for these values is a more than adequate compensation for faith in a supernatural helper, savior, or judge.

All social institutions, including the church, must be progressively but determinedly transformed toward expressing and giving full scope to these values.

In 1945, at the time of my ordination, there was considerable fusillading within Unitarian and Universalist ranks between our liberal Christian theists and our humanists. In both groups there were firebrands who viewed one another as deadening or dangerous to the task of revitalizing liberal religion. In retrospect, the controversy, though awkward, cleared the air. One of those most helpful in a resynthesizing process was the late Dr. Charles E. Park, for many years the eloquent and scholarly minister of Boston's First Church. Park's credentials as a Christian Unitarian were impeccable, so he was listened to when in a sermon he described the prophetic role of humanism as

> a protest against unprofitable speculation concerning matters
> which, by their very nature, lie beyond the reach of human

comprehension; and an appeal to philosophy to give the first freshness of its vigor to problems that fall within its scope. It appears periodically in the history of thought, to keep philosophy within its proper bounds. When scribes, rabbis, and Pharisees in Palestine could find nothing better to do than to get themselves all snarled up in useless conjectures as to the meaning and scope of their precious Law, Jesus appeared teaching the importance of considering the dignity of human nature, the potential capabilities of the human spirit

Did Park mean that Jesus was a humanist? Certainly not in the word's strict sense. What Park meant is that Jesus fulfilled the *spirit* of humanism. "We may call Jesus an unconscious Humanist," said Park, "for if you take away the humanistic element in his teachings there is little left." With equal fairness, we could say the same of Spinoza, Adams, and Ruether. Contrary to Alexander Pope's advice, they "presume to scan God" in depth. And they fulfill the spirit of humanism. Humanity is the measure of their moral passion.

I make this point to dispel a confusion that arises from trying to build walls around humanism or theism to separate them sharply and distinctly from one another, as if religious liberals can be faithful to the ideals of humanism only by banishing God from their vocabulary and vice versa. This can happen only when we forget that we are supposed to be a community of open-minded seekers, all of us blessed with independence of mind and spirit, free to arrive at honest convictions without prejudice to our good standing, and deserving respect for the integrity of our motives. These are our distinguishing characteristics, and not whether we choose to call ourselves theists, humanists, or something else.

It may be that I cherish my Unitarian Universalist affiliation most of all because every congregation I have served harbors a mixture of theists and humanists, Christians and non-Christians. They are, in my opinion, exceedingly good for one another. The theist, whether of the Spinoza, Adams, or Ruether type, exemplifies a persistence in the search for God which is by no means lacking in fruitful results. As Park put it: "Gleams and flashes of insight do come from the surrounding darkness, and help to lighten our way through life's maze." The humanist, meanwhile, keeps reminding that the more insistently we turn toward whatever yields to human guidance, the sooner and better we shall know the immense capacities for good of the human spirit.

Here I Stand

It would be ungracious to conclude this chapter without giving my personal faith stance. I will do it briefly because there have been ample intimations of it in the preceding pages.

In 1947, prior to becoming minister of the Unitarian congregation of Rockford, Illinois, I met with their ministerial search committee. Seated beside me was Cousie Fox, a lifelong church member. Hers was the first question. "Are you a humanist or a theist?" My answer was immediate and honest. "Both!" So it was then, and so it remains.

I affirm heart and soul all of humanism's major premises of faith, just as I listed them. In profoundly humanistic terms, I strive to practice and live my religion as the natural functioning of my personhood in pursuit of a full, free, and socially useful life. I believe that we humans are neither saints nor irredeemable sinners. I believe that we can get somewhere better than where we've gotten so far, that we can improve, that we have within ourselves all the capacities for solving the problems we can reasonably expect to solve. I believe that faith's most critical role is to inspire and strengthen attitudes that will bring humans to the fullest possible consciousness of their freedom, their reason, their aesthetic depths, and their moral capabilities. The joy of comradeship and community in this quest is more than adequate compensation for my nonexistent faith in a supernatural helper, savior, or judge.

I am not willing, however, to abandon imaginary interactions between myself and an ultimate something else in nature which is called God or, now, God/ess. I would not insist that the name *must* be given and indeed, I use it sparingly. There is in me a deep distaste for the slovenly, exploitative ways in which it is merchandised by pulpiteers and politicians. Also, I am concerned that associations of the term with the supernatural are so widespread that any use of it is certain to give rise to misconceptions and be taken as a concession to traditional ideas.

I am a devout believer in applying the experimental method to theology, as well as to physics, chemistry, and musical composition. Down the centuries, questions about the existence and nature of God have been answered with abstractions dictated by cramped theories of knowledge. Immobilized by a long-standing dualism of the mind and its object, thought could conceive of God only as an object separate from humans. Thus, God must be either a figment of the human mind or an Other beyond the reach of human understanding, except through revelation. If God is inaccessible to the human mind, the religiously inclined have only two logical paths open to them. They may become thoroughgoing humanists, content with a conclusion that God is, at present, unknown or unknowable. Or, confessing the inability of philosophy to verify God's existence, they may seek a direct experience of God in the self, in nature, or in a revelation that is of a different order than human reason and knowledge. This was Kant's response to philosophical frustration, and it has been the basis of many theologies since.

The experimental approach to the inquiry centers on actual, observable human experience and asks what this tells us about the nature of God. It is impossible to do this without exploring the history of religions. From such an exploration it becomes clear that the lesser and greater gods of all religions have been the life process itself, idealized and personified. All gods are clothed in the habits and moral codes of their worshippers and invariably reflect the changes that influence the customs, outlooks, and goals of their people. When the followers are warlike, the god is warlike; when the followers are peace loving, the god is peace loving; when the people live under a king, the god is a monarch; when the believers (as among the Enlightenment worthies) espouse and promote democratic ideals, their god underwrites freedom, reason, and justice. Thus God, at all times and in all places, is the spirit of a people as they experience and interpret their existence. To the extent that the world of humanity is embraced, God is the spirit of humanity. Insofar as the universe is consciously conceived as a unity, God is the spirit of the universe.

The prophets of ancient Israel foretold that as humanity's splintered segments achieve a greater sense of commonality, God emerges as truly the Lord of all, with universal commandments of righteousness, justice, mercy, and love. Indeed, as commerce, art, science, and moral interchange level the barriers of human isolation, this is increasingly so. Even so, nationalism, sectarianism, racism, and ethnicity stubbornly and aggressively prevail. At root, God is still conceived of as the soul of particular communal values, particular social traditions, particular loves and hates.

The advantage of such an overview—to say nothing of its existential truth—is that philosophical frustrations about God's "existence" are no longer involved. If the world is a reality, then so is the God who is the living experience, in one form or another, of all people in the world. Whatever reality there is in the lives of individuals, clans, nations, or humanity is imparted in kind and degree to God, and with the flourishing of feminist theology, to God/ess. I readily grant that the total reality of God is greater than any individual's or group's experience of it to date, which is what is so challenging to me about the continuing quest.

Now positively: God, to me, is the Spirit of a spiritual universe in which I share with all life an interdependent destiny. God is that ultimate reality that interacts with all my doings and strivings, both instinctive and intelligent and, in the end, quite literally determines to what degree they are responsible for conserving, transmitting, rectifying, and expanding those values, which alone can redeem and preserve the human community. God enfolds and permeates the so-called material world in which the conditions and actions of living occur. Thus, God is both transcendent as creativity and immanent as the creative event. God, in brief, is the glorious sum of the living process, in which I, as a person, and we, as a human community, live, strive, and die. God is the existence I share with all that is or is to be. God is Being lifted to the utmost limits of my spiritual insight and exertion. God is as genuine as my own nature and as boundless as my most imaginative hopes for spiritual enlightenment. With every deepening of my insight, every strengthening of my moral will, every expansion of my understanding of truth, every experience of beloved community, God is better known to me, more reverently loved, more personally and profoundly experienced.

What the Unitarian Universalist fellowship offers me is the encouragement to be utterly my most responsible self in matters of theological belief. When I use the word *God* or *God/ess*, it is with the full understanding that I speak from personal conviction and experience, and not from any desire to impose my "revelation" on others. By the same token, I not only speak as conscience dictates, but I also listen to what others are saying with an eagerness that comes from wanting to catch the gleams and flashes of their intimations of spirit. Thus does my experience of God increase.

With Their Own Eyes

Some beliefs are like walled gardens. They encourage ex-
clusiveness, and the feeling of being especially privileged.
Other beliefs are expansive and lead the way into wider
and deeper sympathies.

SOPHIA LYON FAHS

Of all the good reasons I can list for being a Unitarian Universalist,
none is more personally exciting to me than our work with children and youth. Over the years, it has seemed to me that new and
better ways of religious learning and growth are coming into
being. The reason is plain: The individual child, rather than a
Bible or catechism, is at the center of our concern, which means
that we are forever challenged to examine and improve what we
are doing. Are our efforts "expansive" enough? Do they "lead the
way into wider and deeper sympathies?" The director for religious
education of the Unitarian Universalist Association, citing the
radical Catholic educator Thomas Groome as his inspiration, describes this as "a process of reflection upon action, a process which
invites one to name one's own knowing, invites deep exploration
of how one came to that knowing, provides challenge with visions
and stories of one's own faith tradition, adds the best insights of
one's own day, moves from that vision to the reality of one's own

life, invites a dialectic among the ideas and a dialog within the church community, and leads one to answer the question, 'What will I do now?' It leads always to action and again to reflection" (Berry Street lecture, by Eugene Navias, 1983).

The Bible is a significant part of our curriculum, but only as it contributes to the broader goals of religious learning and growth for the children entrusted to our care, *and* for the adults to whom that care is entrusted. Let me explain.

Some time ago, a stranger telephoned me and, without preliminaries, asked: "Is the Bible God's own word, or just a bunch of fairy tales?" Feeling that a minister's task is kindliness even toward the belligerent, I answered in my most considerate manner that I believed the Bible to be neither God's own word nor a bunch of fairy tales. I could not tell at that point whether my caller was a divine-inspiration or fairy-tale partisan. "It's got to be one or the other!" he said, providing the semanticist in me with another classic example of the excluded middle. "If it isn't God's word, then it's just a bunch of fairy tales." As it turned out, this particular examiner of my theology was a divine revelationist, bent on giving me yet another chance to mend my ways and save my soul. But he might well have been a zealot of the other school.

In working with the religious learning and growth of children, we recognize first of all that the Bible is no simple either/or matter. We live in a complicated climate of opinion about the Bible. At one extreme are those who despise the Bible for its violence, superstition, and chauvinism. For them, it is an emotionally loaded symbol, just as it is for "true Biblical believers." Only they would just like to get rid of it. To those who feel this way, I can only say that, like it or not, the Bible is a major source of our ideas, habits, and attitudes. From it have come many of our laws, social institutions, morals, and folkways—good and bad. It is a factor in our lives to be dealt with sensibly, feelingly, and intelligently. To reject it out of hand is to betray an emotional ignorance of the enormous spectrum of human experience the Bible contains.

At the opposite pole are those to whom the Bible is the Word, with a capital *W*, of God, with a capital *G*—verbally inspired by God the Father, dictated by God the Holy Ghost, and revealing through God the Son, without jot or tittle of error, the divine scheme of eternal salvation. This view is filled with arrogance. Those who refuse to accept it are immediately labeled as reeking with sin. Its purveyors speak to the needs of untold millions of biblical certainty seekers. A Moral Majority leader in the Midwest encourages his followers to conduct search-and-destroy missions for books in their local libraries that are anti-Bible. "If they . . . feel like burning them, fine," he says. A pastor in Michigan uses a home-made "electric stool" and a twelve-volt battery to shock his young Bible students into "hearing God's word."

From time to time I deliberately practice the hair shirt spiritual discipline of forcing myself to watch some of the celebrated television evangelists preach their biblical fundamentalism and right-wing politics. Via the electronic church, backed by state-of-the-art computerized mailings, they have made a quantum leap, both in reaching mass markets and raising funds. According to my own count, the total audience to which Jesus preached did not exceed twenty thousand persons. Today's electronic preachers speak regularly to millions. One of them, Dr. Oral Roberts, Bible in hand, recently reported to viewers that Jesus had appeared to him in a vision; the vision was "about nine hundred feet tall"; Jesus lifted the unfinished Tulsa hospital Roberts is building high in the air and simultaneously promised that funds would be forthcoming to complete the structure. After sharing his vision with his followers, by direct mail as well as by television, Roberts received almost $5 million in donations, which works out to approximately $5,555 per foot for a nine-hundred-foot Jesus.

Some of this money comes from corporate and individual angels, but more impressive are the amounts that come from tens of thousands of persons and families of modest means and with a deep need to have the supernatural qualities of Holy Writ affirmed. A Methodist minister I knew used to call this a "wooden-headed way of handling the Bible" that was "responsible for a bibically illiterate generation." So, this is a concern that many non-fundamentalist Christians and Jews share with Unitarian Universalists, yet how tardy and hesitant is the carrying over of this concern into the religious education of children. For the most part, churches and synagogues continue in the old way, identifying religious education with the teaching of the Scriptures just as though we still believed them to be an infallible revelation, continue to indoctrinate young minds with certain beliefs regarded as necessary to salvation and to surround those beliefs with an emotional pattern of fear and hope whose purpose is to keep children bound to those dogmas when they are grown. However well intentioned this may be, it remains, in my view, a tragic mistake. It serves neither the best interests of the children, nor the best interests of the adult community of which these children are destined to become members.

What has happened to bring about the changed attitude toward the Bible described by my Methodist minister friend? What has happened to deepen the concern of Unitarian Universalist families about *how* the Bible is used in the religious education of children? The basic answers, of course, are the fruits of biblical scholarship and a revolutionized view of what constitutes religious "learning" for a child. For a century and a half, scholars have devoted their lives to intensive critical studies of the Bible, steadily discovering more about its origins, texts, and contexts. How many laypersons know the meaning of the word *Bible*? It is an English rendering of a Greek word describing the inner bark of a reed which was once used as paper. The plural of this word, *ta biblia*, was used by early Greek-speaking Christians to characterize their most revered writings and simply meant "the books." Later, Latin translators mistakenly used the singular in place of the plural and thus launched the erroneous impression that the Bible is a single, unified book.

In medieval times, scribes attempted to correct the error by using another word, *bibliotheca*, which means "library." They were justified in this, because the Bible is a collection of books, a library, which does not express a single theme but encompasses a diversity of subject matters. For example, the gloomy, sophisticated, skeptical viewpoint of the author of Ecclesiastes clashes sharply with the cosmic optimism of Isaiah. They write of two different world views and two different sets of spiritual experiences. Existence is morally meaningless to one, full of moral meaning to the other. Yet, there they are in the same Bible, both canonized. The explanation is that the books of the Bible were written over a millennium by authors of widely divergent outlooks and purposes. It is not at all unnatural that the Book of Judges varies profoundly from the Book of James in moral stance and tone.

Another simple historical fact, known by surprisingly few, is that the earliest Christians had no scriptures of their own. There was, as yet, no "New" Testament; consequently there was no "Old" Testament either. The first Christian Bible was the Jewish Bible, the Torah, which was Jesus's Bible as well. First- and second-generation Christians lived in eager anticipation of the return of Jesus the Christ, the Anointed One, the Messiah. Since the Savior was soon to mount his throne as ruler of earth, there was little reason to add to the existing holy books of the Jews. It was enough to tell and retell the wonder stories of Jesus by word of mouth. When congregations gathered for religious services, there would be recitations from the Jewish Scriptures, with additional renderings of Paul's letters and those of other apostles.

A fair summary of what scholarship tells us about Jewish Scripture is that we are dealing with a wonderfully diversified product of nearly a thousand years of a people's religious and cultural development. What emerges from a painstaking sifting of Genesis, Exodus, Leviticus, Numbers, and Deuteronomy is a patchwork accomplished by editors who combined primitive folklore and myth with legendary accounts of how the Hebrew tribes came into existence and developed into a nation. There are ancient legal codes and manuals of hygiene, early battle songs and poems, of which the Song of Deborah may well be the oldest recorded material in the Bible. All of this is woven by succeeding generations of editors into an epic story.

The original authors of the myths, legends, traditions, and histories are unknown. The later editors are unknown. We do know, however, that the cutting and pasting process went on for several hundred years. We also know that during this period the Hebrews emerged from primitive forms of religion, such as magic arks and animal sacrifices, to much more elevated forms, and that this advancement can be plainly traced through the Jewish Scriptures. Some eight hundred years before Jesus, there arose among the Hebrews those remarkable reformers known as the prophets. In all, these Scriptures contain a dozen brief prophetic books, the long Isaiah (which is actually several books) and the two major works attributed to Jeremiah. By this time the Hebrew religion had evolved into monotheism and produced an inspired ethical universalism, of which the prophets were the formulators and articulators.

The collection of Hebrew holy books, this fantastic library of the Jewish experience, was translated into Greek for the use of dispersed Greek-speaking Jewish communities scattered over the Mediterranean region. It was taken up by the early Christian congregations and adopted as their own. In this manner it was subjected to the re-interpretations that made it over into a familiar segment of the Christian salvation story.

As the years rolled on and the certainty of Christ's imminent return faded, there arose, understandably, a need for Scriptures that were distinctly Christian. The churches were fractured by internal conflicts and disputes, even as they were oppressed by persecution. The authority and inspiration of Scriptures of "the new dispensation" were required. Appeals were made to the letters of Paul and others. Reverence for the remembered teachings and wonder works of Jesus was transformed into a demand for permanent, authoritative accounts. Unhappily for us, the earliest texts of these memoirs are lost. They did, however, form the basis of what we have: the Gospels of what Christians insisted was the *New* Testament, automatically relegating the Hebrew Scriptures to the status of Old.

Still, we remain much in the dark, for the original manuscripts of the Gospels have never been found. We possess only relatively late translations and copies of material that was first written down long after Jesus. There are formidable problems of textual and historical interpretation.

What we do know is that three of the Gospels (Matthew, Mark, and Luke) are based on two primary sources: a collection of the sayings of Jesus, which Matthew and Luke treat in different ways, and an earlier form of Mark's Gospel. The Gospel of John is regarded by most scholars as historically less accurate. It was composed much later than the other three and is less factual. It is impossible to reconcile the Gospel of John with its counterparts.

Reverence for the collection of works now known as the New Testament steadily increased. But there were also tensions. Some church leaders were suspicious of books that might outstrip their personal authority, but at the same time, the bishops, as they had come to be called, recognized the need for written works to consolidate their power, as well as to inform the faithful. The dilemma was solved by claiming that the added volumes were really a part of the Sacred Scriptures—a *New* Testament as distinguished from the Old—and that only the properly designated authorities of the Church could interpret it.

Even with so brief and sketchy an introduction as this, the question of whether the Bible is a book dictated by God becomes facetious. The Bible is replete with inaccuracies, inconsistencies, and errors, which should surprise no one in so great a compendium, compiled over a millennium from numberless sources, authors, editors, and copyists. The Bible is a saga not of one religion but of many, some of which exist side by side. I recently led a workshop called "The Nine Religions of the Bible" for my Bedford, Massachusetts, congregation. It turned out to be an exciting and informative way of starting with Genesis and ending with Revelation and making some sense of an evolutionary whole.

Basically it is a bit unfair to attribute this aggregate to God. The Bible was inspired bit by bit and part by part by the experiences of people over centuries. An obvious extension of this is that scripture is still being written and will continue to be written as long as there are men and women who are spiritually sensitive to what is happening to them and their world. It is much better to accept the Judeo-Christian Bible for its uniqueness as a library of ancient human experience and to know and love it for this, than to surround it with a supernatural aura. The inspiration of the real Bible is wisdom distilled from struggle and insight gained from the hard evolution of human life. The Bible makes just claims upon us, not in terms of divine authorship, but on the basis of the everlasting quest for the redeemed life and the assurance that humans, in their search for deeper meanings and larger purposes, must progress from lesser to greater truths.

We Unitarian Universalists include the Bible in our learning and growth programs for children, youth, and adults, but we take special care with children. There are many good stories, words of wisdom, and inspiring thoughts in the Bible. Knowing more about them from a historical perspective helps our children to express and defend their own developing beliefs. Ours is a culture deeply, if often confusingly, permeated by the Judeo-Christian tradition. Anyone who does not know anything about David or Ruth or Jesus or Mary and Martha is culturally illiterate. That's not playing fair with our young. They deserve, at the very least, to have their curiosity stimulated about the legends, myths, stories, teachings, and symbols that pervade our culture.

The care we exercise is to encourage our children to approach the Bible with unawed candor, on the assumption that it was written by human beings like ourselves. The care we exercise with ourselves as parents and other adult mentors is twofold: First, we are genuine about overcoming our own biblical illiteracy; second, we respect the ability of children to grasp only what they have the capacity to understand and absorb, and this is limited by age level and development. We do not try to infiltrate the religious consciousness of a second-grader with all of the profound issues of the Book of Job, yet a second-grader can wrestle with the fundamental fact that bad things do happen to good people, and vice versa.

Unitarian Universalist parents sometimes look longingly at

the supposed biblical literacy drilled into the heads of children in traditional Sunday schools. But the results can be startling. One study I am familiar with was of a group of fifty college sophomores, selected on the basis of demonstrated scholastic aptitude and achievement. The students had experienced Bible training as children in either orthodox Protestant or Catholic churches. They were then given a five-week refresher course followed by an examination, which demonstrated that only eight or nine had anything resembling a solid knowledge of the Bible. The rest were swamped in confusion. They had no real conception of the differences between the Hebrew and Christian Scriptures. Many thought that Jesus appears in both. Some thought Jesus gave the Ten Commandments to Moses. A few thought he was Job's companion. The prevailing sentiment was that everything in the Bible happened at about the same time and in the same place. Most thought of the Bible as teaching a single, clear ethical code throughout. The majority, in spite of massive confusion about its contents, insisted that the Bible was to be accepted as a whole. There were no marked differences between Protestant and Roman Catholic students.

The only possible conclusion from this particular study, and it is borne out by others, is that the undiscriminating goal of simply "teaching the Bible" can do more harm than good. Given the approach widely used, it cannot be otherwise. In Unitarian Universalist programs of religious learning and growth, biblical materials are delicately and discriminatingly used with children, not because we want to deprive them of biblical knowledge and inspiration, but because we want them to have a chance, gradually and developmentally, to know the Bible as it is. We believe this can happen only incrementally, with the best results emerging at the upper age levels, and only if parents and families join wholeheartedly in the process with ministers, directors of religious education, and church school teachers.

I have the benefit of a good deal of continuing education in the literature of the Bible. My own earlier jumble of misinformation has long since been unscrambled, so it is no longer easy for me to re-experience that jumble in the midst of my exposure to a conventional Sunday school. But by the gift of imagination, I can lay out a likely scenario. Once upon a time, a white-bearded giant named God, who lived in the sky but sometimes visited the earth, told a king to kill everybody except his own relatives (the story of Samuel, Saul, and the Amalekites), and at about the same time God was telling a man named Noah to build a great ship in which to save his family and two of each kind of animal (because God was going to drown everyone else) and that there was a man named Jesus living in the same place who taught that God loved everybody but was still going to burn all the bad people. (It is worth noting that children are aware of the fact that they are often "bad.")

My heart goes out to youngsters who are "learning" that the good Jesus and the savage David were both faithful servants of God, and that tricky Jacob was a favorite of God and was rewarded, while the good Jesus was allowed to die on a cross, and that God slew all the first-born children of Egypt because the Egyptian ruler was quarreling with Moses.

Exaggerated as I make it sound, this is precisely the kind of problem we face when it comes to teaching the Bible indiscriminately to children. Think of all the little ones who have been taught this way and have never gotten over it.

We are not likely to repeat this error in Unitarian Universalist religious education, because we are concerned first with the child's spiritual development and not with a hasty administration of biblical salvation. We want our children to know and appreciate the Bible for what it is, and we are determined that, to the best of our ability, they will have access to the kind of knowing and understanding they can later trust and respect.

Here is how we might undertake this task in any one of our church schools, with the expectation, of course, of cooperation at home. To five- and six-year-olds we introduce for discussion some of the simplest Bible stories, such as the Passover and Christmas legends, and some of the most familiar teachings, such as the

Golden Rule. With seven- and eight-year-olds we begin to make use of educationally sound Bible storybooks such as the story of Joseph with its dramatic human interest as a family-centered tale of jealousy, achievement, and forgiveness. We encourage the children to act out the religious legends and myths of many different peoples in addition to those of the Bible.

Nine- and ten-year-olds may become acquainted with the creation stories of Genesis (there are two, not, as popularly believed, one) and have an opportunity to compare them with other creation stories and with scientific theories of the universe.

At the age of eleven and twelve, youngsters are ready for their first serious probes of the life and teachings of Jesus. As teenagers, they can begin to fill in backgrounds for Jesus in the historical drama of ancient Israel and become familiar with the great prophets and their ethical concerns. High school students are encouraged to come of age with deeper first-hand explorations of their own Unitarian Universalist heritage and the roles in that of Judaism, Jesus, the beginnings of Christianity, and the practices of various Christian groups.

Throughout this process, our young participate in services of celebration and worship, often intergenerational. Particularly at high holiday times—Rosh Hashanah, Christmas, Easter—these services embrace biblical stories, rituals, symbols, and songs.

Please understand that I have been writing only of the dimension of our approach to children's religious learning and growth that deals specifically with the Bible. I have done so at some length to clarify, as well, prevalent adult Unitarian Universalist perceptions and understandings of the Bible. There is far, far more than the Bible in our religious education efforts as a whole. Our fundamental concern in religious learning and growth for children is that they have a foundation of understanding, awakened interest, and enriched experience to appreciate not only the Bible, as they become really capable of comprehending it, but also many other founts of spiritual inspiration as well.

The Great End in Religious Instruction

I honor the sincerity of those traditional Christian communions whose approach to religious education rests on human nature's alienation from God, with reunion possible only by learning and internalizing a doctrinal plan of salvation. Children, according to this view, must be taught the saving revelation, which alone can rescue them from inherited original sin.

Religious education in Unitarian Universalist circles is founded on the conviction that human nature, rather than alienating us from God, binds us to the universe and to all that sustains it. The human nature of children is neither inherently wicked nor inherently good. It is potentially both. Within the natural needs, urges, impulses, drives, and curiosity of children is the very stuff of which a religious education should be fashioned. We are respectful of the degree to which "genes are destiny." We are enthusiastic about the degree to which children, as a crucial portion of their genetic destiny, are natural and creative learners—unless and until their natural and creative bent is stifled and destroyed.

What we strive to offer children is loving, informed nurture for achieving a religion, a spirituality that is truly their own and is shareable. If our young are to have a religion of their own, we of the liberal religious community must do everything in our power to teach by example, as well as by precept. We must demonstrate that all of us are about the business of discovering religion for ourselves.

"Thou shalt love thy neighbor as thyself." This is the kind of injunction children have been memorizing in Sunday schools for generations. But if the premise is that the child is lost until saved by grace, conversion, and creedal belief, what possible meaning can the injunction have? It is a simple reality that you cannot love your neighbor effectively if you feel contempt for self, if you cannot, dare not, and have not the freedom to trust and respect yourself. Unless girls and boys are able to believe that they are worth loving, there is no logic in expecting them to love their neighbors. To help our children to build an awareness of their own worth, and thus to create a genuine foundation for respecting the worth

of others, is one of our supreme aims in religious education—
from the cradle on.

In Herb Gardner's play *A Thousand Clowns*, the central character, Murray, tells what he wants for a young nephew who has
been left in his care:

> I want him to be sure he'll know when he's chickening out on
> himself. I want him to get to know exactly the special thing he
> is or else he won't notice when it starts to go. I want him to
> stay awake and know who the phonies are. I want him to
> know how to holler and put up an argument. I want a little
> guts to show before I can let him go. I want to be sure he sees
> all the wild possibilities. . . . And I want him to know the sub-
> tle, sneaky, important reason why he was born a human being
> and not a chair.

Murray's passionate words go to the heart of what religious education means to us, with this significant addition: One of the most
important reasons for being born a human being and not a chair
is to learn the wonders of community—of practicing mutuality,
interdependence, and involvement. Otherwise Murray is right on
target, expressing what I want for my children and yours, for my
grandchildren and yours. It is what I want for every child in the
congregation I serve, for every child in the world. It is what I want
for myself, and for you.

A key clue to what Unitarian Universalist religious education is up
to is that a child's religion grows out of natural, not supernatural,
experience. Religion is not something "revealed" to a child, or
thrust upon a child; it is something to be nurtured and encouraged in a child's unfolding life. We believe that spirituality will
grow naturally out of a child's everyday living and maturing,
which is why we emphasize the enrichment of experiences in the
here and now rather than confining ourselves to rehearsals of the
deeds of Jesus and other biblical worthies. We believe that young

people are ready for direct, immediate experiences of birth, growth, death, nature, love, hate, joy, and suffering—the fierce yet wondrous ambiguities of life.

Out of such experiences come the beginnings of religion. We believe that a primary order of business of the teaching and learning congregation is to help children to articulate such experiences in their own words and ways, *before* their minds have been frozen by adult explanations. Instead of being taught to memorize traditional prayers and litanies for the sole reason of repeating them parrotlike, our children are encouraged to recognize and respect the Lord's Prayer, for example, and the Twenty-third Psalm. But more important, they are encouraged to speak of their awes, enthusiasms, fears, and questionings in their own unconstrained way. Heartening youngsters to search the mysteries of their here-and-now experiences is to us the soundest beginning of a religion that will deepen and mature. All along the way, as they become ready for it, their searchings can be profitably and excitingly compared to those of an Isaiah, a Jesus, a Sojourner Truth, or a Gandhi.

A century and a half ago, William Ellery Channing did a remarkable job of formulating the aims of methods of liberal religious education as it applies to the young at home and at church. His insight continues to serve as a reality check whenever we slip into purely secular means of achieving religious goals. Channing wrote:

> The great end in religious instruction, whether in the Sunday School or family, is, not to stamp our minds irresistibly on the young, but to stir up their own; not to make them see with our eyes, but to look inquiringly and steadily with their own; not to give them a definite amount of knowledge, but to inspire a fervent love of truth; not to form an outward regularity, but to quicken and strengthen the power of thought; not to bind them by ineradicable prejudices to our particular sect or peculiar notions, but to prepare them for impartial, conscientious judging of whatever subjects may, in the course of Providence, be offered to their decision; not

to impose religion upon them in the form of arbitrary rules which rest on no foundation but our own word and will, but to awaken the consciousness, the moral discernment, so that they may discern and approve for themselves what is ever-lastingly right and good (*The Sunday School Discourse*).

One can readily see why this statement still stands both as a reminder of our inevitable shortcomings and as the ideal for which we strive.

Our children are not, cannot, and should not be quarantined from traditional and orthodox religious beliefs. They are bound to bump into them head-on among their playmates, to say nothing of relatives, babysitters, and born-again Christian teachers. This is an inevitable complication in guiding a child's religious development along liberal lines, but it is also an opportunity.

My colleague, Tony Larsen, who left a Roman Catholic order to take up studies for the Unitarian Universalist ministry, has a unique perspective:

Believe me, most UU children I know would *not* have been a match for me when I was a kid. When I was young I went around the neighborhood spreading the fear of hell and the wrath of God; and was I good at it. Sometimes I'd walk around in my little priest outfit and sprinkle holy water here and there. And sometimes I'd invite the other kids to come to the church my dad built for me in the back-yard, and I'd tell them all about the Catholic religion. If the kids were Catholic but not going to church, I'd remind them of the hell-fire awaiting them if they should die. And if the kids were Protestant, I'd tell them that being Protestant didn't *automatically* keep them out of heaven, but it sure made it difficult to get there. I mean, I was the kind of kid that most Unitarian Universalist parents try to protect their children from.

The point Larsen makes is this: Yes, we want our children to make their own religious choices, to develop naturally a religious faith anchored in their own experience. No, we don't want to push beliefs on them, or shove our religion down their throats. Yes, we want our children to grow up spiritually free. "That's nice," he says, "and I agree. But that doesn't mean that you can't give a plug for your religion . . . you can at least *share* your beliefs with them." Larsen sadly concludes, with considerable intergenerational experience, that many Unitarian Universalist young people "do *not* know what their parents believe about God, and afterlife and Christianity. And most parents don't know what their *kids* believe. . . . Is it too much heresy to suggest that you sit down together and talk about your beliefs? That's not shoving your religion down their throats. Sharing is a little different from shoving."

Larsen's plea touches a sensitive nerve, and deserves to. Our philosophy of religious education represents a revolutionary departure from traditional Sunday school techniques.

We do not teach a finished gospel. But that doesn't mean we are bereft of convictions and devotions that give direction to our lives and are shareable with our young. I have filled these pages with convictions and devotions we have in common.

We do everything possible to avoid an atmosphere in which children might feel that their natural curiosity is being repressed. But isn't it a natural part of their curiosity to want to know why our church commitment is powerfully attractive to us, and why we might reasonably hope that they will choose to remain Unitarian Universalists when they grow up, though we'll go right on loving them whether they do or not?

We never suggest that truth, beauty, and goodness are to be cherished simply because they are honored in our church and our religion. But they are honored in our church, which is going to need people like them to keep up the honoring. There's no reason our young shouldn't be helped to know how to put up an argument when they are challenged on the street, or in the classroom, or at the beach, about being headed for hell because of their beliefs and their church affiliation. In Tony Larsen's words: "If *you* don't prepare your kids in religion, there may be a little Tony Larsen in your neighborhood who *will*."

We are enjoying a dynamic time of rebirth in Unitarian Universalist religious education: more children and youth, more families, more trained ministers and directors, new curriculum and teaching guides. And there is a new emphasis as well, one that says the entire program of a liberal church should be considered an adventure in religious learning and growth. Perhaps this is best described as a holistic approach. It gives equal emphasis to children and adults. It gives equal emphasis to worship, fellowship, social action, and education. The old model of religious education as a "school" for children, while the adults worship, is giving way to one in which religious learning and growth take place in the context of the religious community as a whole. We are increasingly convinced that our religious communities are strengthened by the creative interchange of people of all ages who share deeply with one another and, to the greatest extent possible, do their religious growing and learning in one another's presence. Eugene Navias, in his 1983 Berry Street lecture, expresses it this way:

> I would hold that for each of us to be fully human is to be using our endowment for growth throughout our lifespan, that to be fully human is to be developing our complementary human capacities of the spirit, soul, reason, passion, imagination and intuition in ways which lead to our greatest liberation and most just action. To be fully human is to get our powers together to become most integrated, whole, and in that sense, "religious."

Parents who think they can put their children in Sunday school for one or two hours a week to "get" religious education will not be comfortable in one of our churches. Our outreach is to those who wish to enter *with* their children (if they have them, if not, with the children of others) upon an adventure in lifelong religious learning and growth. Should this strike a responsive chord, make contact with your nearest Unitarian Universalist congregation.

In all of this we have tried not to overlook individuals and families who live at too great a distance from a Unitarian

Universalist church or who are homebound. For them there is our Church of the Larger Fellowship, with headquarters, a minister, and a religious education director at 25 Beacon Street, Boston, MA 02108, which sends religious education materials, books, sermons, and a regular newsletter to all who affiliate with this imaginative outreach to the isolated.

If Channing set the course for Unitarian Universalist religious education with his memorable 1837 address to the Sunday School Society, Sophia Lyon Fahs did more than any other individual in this century to steer us toward the tangible fulfillment of his hopes. She died a few years ago after a long, productive life of bringing into being the resources, curricular and human, for contemporary liberal religious education. The enduring quality of her inspiration is best exemplified in her own words:

> Some beliefs are like blinders, shutting off the power to choose one's own direction. Other beliefs are like gateways opening wide vistas for exploration. Some beliefs weaken a person's selfhood. They blight the growth of resourcefulness. Other beliefs nurture self-confidence and enrich the feeling of personal worth. Some beliefs are rigid, like the body of death, impotent in a changing world. Other beliefs are pliable, like the young sapling, ever growing with the upward thrust of life (*Today's Children and Yesterday's Heritage*).

Taking the Time to Care

> We are learning that a standard of social ethics is not attained by traveling a sequestered byway, but by mixing on the thronged and common road where all must turn out for one another, and at least see the size of one another's burdens.
>
> JANE ADDAMS

"Why are you doing this?" The year was 1947 and my questioner was dean of the faculty of the medical school in Vienna. World War II was over, but its gruesome reminders were everywhere. We were sitting in a three-hundred-year-old room of Vienna's bullet-riddled central hospital. The day's surgery and seminar sessions were ended. I was there as secretary to a team of prominent American and Swiss physicians sponsored by the Unitarian Service Committee (later merged with the Universalist Service Committee to become the Unitarian Universalist Service Committee). Our purpose was to do all we could to provide Austrian doctors with the latest skills and techniques in medicine and surgery. The once-proud center of the healing arts had suffered terribly from the ravages of Nazism and war. The Unitarian Service Committee, with the full cooperation of the newly established democratic government of Austria, the World Health Organization, and the four-power military occupation, had organized a mission of twelve specialists to act as midwives at the rebirth of Austrian medicine.

"Why are you doing this?" the dean asked. Earlier he had quizzed me about the religious interests of the twelve team-members. He raised his eyebrows when I told him that only two of the doctors were Unitarians, and that was quite by happenstance. "Do you expect to get Unitarian converts by this program?" he asked. I told him that we only wanted to do something useful for Austrians. "The work of the Service Committee is entirely non-sectarian," I explained. "Why are you doing this?" he inquired, shaking his head.

For most Unitarian Universalists, religion means little if it does not include enlightened conscience in action. We continually remind ourselves that the word *ethics* is shorthand for actions arising out of faith and from within community. Or, as Jane Addams put it: "To attain individual morality in an age demanding social morality . . . is utterly to fail to apprehend the situation." Yet, we are not missionary minded. We send no missionaries over the face of the earth to convert others to our way of believing. In fact, as I explained, we generally feel that people of other religions have as much to teach us as we have to teach them.

We have the moral equivalents of missionary activities, one of the most dramatic of which is the Unitarian Universalist Service Committee (UUSC). Independent of the Unitarian Universalist Association, the UUSC works in close harmony with it and shares the same basic, supportive constituency. Established in 1940 to rescue Jewish and other refugees from Nazi Europe, the UUSC has kept pace with the changing needs of our changing times. Kindled by compassionate imagination and fanned by a desire to share skills, resources, and goodwill with people the world around, it has carried out, over the years, a remarkable array of programs ranging from direct assistance for victims of war, repression, and hunger to community development and advocacy projects at home and abroad.

We support the work of the Service Committee and participate as volunteers in it because it represents our profound spiritual need to mingle "on the thronged and common road where all must turn out for one another, and at least see the size of one another's burdens." We do not expect anyone to pat us on the head for being "good," and we do not expect anyone to become "converted" in return. We work *with* and not just *for* others. If it is possible for us to bring help, or know-how, or advocacy, or whatever where it is needed, we want to try to meet the need, but only in keeping with what others express to be their desires. We never try to impose a project on unwilling recipients.

We have consistently tried to adjust our programs to changing world patterns. We sincerely try not to succumb to the temptation to tell people what they ought to be doing. Our ability to work is stringently circumscribed by funds made available through voluntary contributions and grants, so it is of the utmost importance that we choose wisely among the overwhelming needs of an age of revolutionary change and disruption. We have learned the dangers of entering into a tug of war for the affections of people on the basis of who offers the better handouts. Our projects are never conceived of as competition or as bringing the "light" of salvation. We only wish to join hands with people struggling for their own lives and dignity. By so doing we feel that we are demonstrating to ourselves that religion is far more than a Sunday morning gesture to God. Behind the UUSC there is a powerful religious motivation, but it is not one of seeking converts. It is the motivation of demonstrating that mutuality is the way to One World, One Humanity.

Strength and Promise

As a nation, the United States views itself as the greatest example of power and plenty the world has ever known. Yet, in the midst of our vaunted technological millennium, we walk daily on the brink of a catastrophe so great that we can hardly grasp its possible consequences. Nor is the threat of nuclear holocaust the only symptom of distress in our otherwise upbeat and affluent way of life. The economic cornucopia we prize so highly is mocked by spreading slums, deepening poverty, stubborn racial injustice, a deteriorating environment, a bottomless pit of military expenditures, and a general retreat from compassion both in and out of government. In the world at large, U.S. policies contribute to a distribution of wealth so inequitable that thoughtful people are haunted by the fear of consequences.

The point I want to make about these evils is that, while we generally deplore them, we consistently refuse to recognize our responsibility for them, instead telling ourselves that it is the wicked who are to blame. In World War I it was Kaiser Wilhelm and the Huns. A generation later it was Hitler, Mussolini, Tojo, and Stalin (until he became our wartime ally, after which he reverted to devil status). Hitler, of course, blamed it all on the Jews, with one of history's most hideous results. Today it is blamed on communists (Chinese and Yugoslav varieties currently excepted), among whose secret minions, according to the new religious right, are feminists, liberals, and environmentalists. Some blame it all on the AFL-CIO, others on the military-industrial complex, others on sinful human nature, and still others on "deluded do-gooders." Most of us want desperately to believe in some sort of devil who is responsible for the evils that beset us. Religious fundamentalists have the advantage of being able to blame Satan, while political conservatives can blame the American Civil Liberties Union.

We Unitarian Universalists, if we are true to our conscience and reason, must be content with the uncomfortable truth that we, individually and collectively, create by our own actions and inactions the world in which we live and suffer or rejoice. We know that no class, race, religion, political party, economic system, dictator, or rebel can be absolved from responsibility or singled out as the only villain. So, if we were to get down on our knees and pray, "Oh God, bring peace to our world by helping us to realize that it is *we* who must wage peace, by our attitudes, thoughts, and acts," we could pray with a clear conscience.

Because humans are human and love to blame devils for their difficulties, religions often are sadly ineffective against the world's ills, though this is by no means a fatal flaw in religion. There is in

religion a high tradition concerned with the *all* of life and dedicated to its enhancement. The great Hebrew prophets insisted that
God is concerned with the well-being of *all* peoples. One of the
finest sayings attributed to Jesus is "But whosoever would be great
among you, shall be your helper; and whosoever would be first
among you, shall be servant of all." This principle is applicable to
every kind of human relations: of spouses, parents and children,
teachers and pupils, employers and employees, privileged and un-
derprivileged, and nations. Religion fails, not because of an internal defect, but because it is lived in fallible people. A confession of
faith is never a substitute for responsible action.

Religion may be a matter of prayer, but prayer without responsible action is a mockery. Religious faith may at times be a
necessary retreat from the world, but retreat without a vigorous
return to responsible action is contempt for life.

In the heat of the civil rights struggles of the 1960s I wrote a
book called *The Martyrs: Sixteen Who Gave Their Lives for Racial
Justice.* Ten of the sixteen who died in the cause of civil rights were
black, six were white—eleven men, one woman, four children. All
were murdered in Alabama and Mississippi, by dynamite or by
gun. In gathering the material, I spent many hours talking with
white clergy in the towns and cities where the killings had occurred. Three of the dead, George Lee, James Reeb, and Jonathan
Daniels, had been ministers. I divided the pastors I had inter-
viewed into three groups. There were those who had risked their
all by calling on their congregations to accept desegregation and
to condemn violence. Some had already been fired, others expected the same, and a few thought they could make it through. A
second group were pastors of prestigious parishes. Although most
favored the civil rights cause and abhorred violence, they felt con-
strained to preserve the unity of their congregations by keeping
silent in order "to be effective in the future." The third and largest
group consisted of pastors who, again for the most part, favored
the end of Jim Crow, but who were still dealing with the problem,
as they essentially expressed it, "by praying for guidance," which

seemed to mean praying for guidance on how to say something without being heard.

I do not stand in judgment of these pastors. I am reasonably certain that I would not be found in the third group. But without actually being in that situation and having to make a decision about my personal course, I cannot say with assurance whether I would take my stand with the first group or the second. I can only say where I *hope* I would be found. Those of us who defend religion by relating it to the problems and conditions of life know that the ultimate test is responsible action from which there is no escape when greater and lesser values are in conflict. We know that in order to win a hearing for a worthy concept of religion there is no way of avoiding the pain of choice.

The dismal showing so often made by religious leaders and organized religious groups can be largely attributed to the narrow notion that religion is a system of props and supports for the individual. Actually, I do not contest that this is one of religion's significant and powerful functions. Few of us can do without spiritual support and solace, but a religious expression that turns only inward, that fails to help us face and carry through the moral responsibilities inherent in the economic, political, and social structures, is in decay. Religion's high tradition as a vehicle of deepening social conscience is brought to shame if a church focuses primarily on rituals and "feel good" fellowship. Not that there is anything innately wrong with rituals and "feel good" fellowship. Far from it. But history most honors religionists who, from the depths of their faith and fellowship, cry out against economic and social evils, paint a glowing picture of life as it should be when it is lived in mutual respect and service, and exalt the earth as a sacred trust for all.

Hearing this, one is bound to say: But wait. What can a mere handful do in a world like ours? On many issues we can't even agree among ourselves. How can we expect to do more than learn to live with all the grace and resignation we can muster?

Unitarian Universalists *are* a mere handful. Though our adult membership on the North American continent is increasing at an encouraging pace, we still number only about 140,000 in a huge sea of religious orthodoxy. Child and youth enrollments in our congregations, now gaining substantially, are about to pass the 40,000 mark, but they are only a tiny segment of the whole. With each passing month our membership is growing, but we are still talking of exceedingly modest totals in comparison with the statistics of other major religious bodies. Organized congregations are forming or are soon to be formed in dozens of new locations, adding to the more than 1,000 already dotting the continent's cities and towns. Still, this is nothing when compared with the number of Methodists, Baptists, or Roman Catholics.

In a mere handful, however, there is the power to move mountains, redress grievances, and change the climate of a community. Over the years I have preached scores of sermons at services in which my colleagues were being installed in new ministries. Invariably the participants include local priests, rabbis, and ministers of other denominations, who just as invariably express their gratitude for the tonic effect on the community and their own pastorates of the Unitarian Universalist presence. We are appreciated!

From so small an acorn has grown an amazing oak. Unitarian Universalists at the White House have included John Adams, Thomas Jefferson, John Quincy Adams, Millard Fillmore, and William Howard Taft. Adlai E. Stevenson didn't make it, but there are millions who still wish he had. Seventeen of the seventy-seven Olympians in the U.S. Hall of Fame came from our ranks. Equally impressive is the roll of literary figures: the Longfellows, Oliver Wendell Holmes, Louisa May Alcott, Ralph Cullen Bryan, Margaret Fuller, Edward Everett Hale, Ralph Waldo Emerson, James Russell Lowell, Nathaniel Hawthorne, Bret Harte, and Catharine Sedgewick. Nor should we forget great historians such as George Bancroft, John Lothrop Morley, Francis Parkman, and William Prescott.

Because of our emphasis on service and social change, our movement has produced an amazing number of pioneers. Championing the anti-slavery cause were such figures as Maria Chapman, Lydia Maria Child, and Samuel J. May. Stalwarts for women's rights and human rights in general were Lucy Stone, Judith Sargent Murray, Julia Ward Howe, Elizabeth Cady Stanton, and Susan B. Anthony. In education some of the familiar names are Horace Mann, initiator of universal, nonsectarian, public education; Elizabeth Palmer Peabody, first to establish a kindergarten; Cyrus Pierce, pioneer crusader for teacher training programs; and Peter Cooper, founder of the famed Cooper Union in New York.

We can also include, among the most honored of humanitarians, Joseph Tuckerman, architect of the profession of social work; Dorothea Lynde Dix, whose boundless energies launched reform movements in prisons, charity institutions, and care for the mentally ill; Samuel G. Howe, who founded the first school for the blind; and Henry Bergh who helped establish the Society for the Prevention of Cruelty to Children and founded the American Society for the Prevention of Cruelty to Animals. Others who made memorable application of their religious ideals to public welfare include George William Curtis, pioneer advocate of civil service; Mary Livermore and Henry Bellows, early leaders of the United States Sanitary Commission, which later, under the inspired guidance of Clara Barton, became the Red Cross; and Whitney M. Young, Jr., who led the Urban League to unprecedented growth and effectiveness.

Similar lists could be enumerated of Unitarian Universalists who laid foundations for modern science, medicine, and the arts. These leaders are but a few of the many who justify the pride Unitarian Universalists feel about the influence of our religious movement. It has been all out of proportion to our numbers in moving public opinion forward, initiating social change, and making history. Fortunately we can turn to the present with comparable satisfaction to find a brilliant array of leaders acting as articulators and exemplars of our way of life. Indeed the list is so extensive I beg off from the risk, and the injustice, of singling out a few to the exclusion of the equally deserving many.

The strength of Unitarian Universalism is the strength of those who, though only a relative handful, are determined not to let the complexities of life deaden the imagination to care. The promise of our faith is crisply summarized in the aspiration: Give us the serenity to accept what cannot be changed, the courage to change what can be changed, and the wisdom to know one from the other. Or, as Jesse Jackson puts it: "If you try you *may* fail; if you don't try you're *sure* to fail."

Let me offer two practical examples of how it works when, out of aroused consciences, people say: "Our vision is always incomplete. No matter. We must move from questions we cannot answer to answers we cannot evade."

That's what happened when, on October 15, 1973, the congregation of the First Unitarian Church of Chicago and I, as senior minister, joined thirty other plaintiff organizations and individuals in a class action suit against the Chicago Police Red Squad. The purpose was to lay bare and, hopefully, to abolish the systematic spying done on us and many other lawful religious and secular groups whose "sin" was apparently that of sustained criticism of various aspects of the Richard Daley administration. A major vehicle for this criticism was the Alliance to End Repression, a broad coalition of Chicago-area civic, religious, and community groups that developed as a result of the police execution of Black Panther leaders in December 1969. I was one of the founders of the alliance and served as its first chairperson. My congregation belonged to it and made a significant financial contribution each year to the budget of the alliance, whose overall objective was strict observance of constitutional guarantees coupled with reform of all facets of the judicial system.

Our lawsuit required years of patient, unflappable effort, but had spectacular results. The Red Squad was abolished. We gained access to all of their files in undeleted form, an unprecedented accomplishment. We won a broad federal injunction, which for the first time outlawed political spying by a city's police department and set forth the toughest set of restrictions on intelligence agencies at all levels of government (including the FBI and CIA). A decade later, claims for civil damages resulting from the spying were still being litigated. In 1983, the alliance went back to court to block the implementation of new FBI rules, contending successfully that at least four provisions violate the injunction agreed to in the Red Squad suit. In matters like these, the beat goes on. The need for vigilance is eternal.

How does this costly involvement by congregation and minister reflect my understanding of Unitarian Universalist religious and social principles? For us there is an inescapable, commanding necessity to rebuke arrogant official power and defend freedom of voluntary association. This necessity arises out of our faith in human freedom, reason, and responsibility. It is rooted in our collective memory of the indivisible nature of lawful liberty and the awful consequences of lawless official power. We must assert and insist, by word and deed, that in a democratic society laws must be respected first and foremost by those who make and enforce them.

Is it more important to speak out as an institution, or as an individual? Conscience is individual, but it is also organic and social. Both aspects of conscience are precious in our heritage. But to insist on only going it alone is to fail to grasp the human situation. I believe that, until we roll up our sleeves and join hands as a community of faith, we cannot fully experience the redemptive power of our convictions or our witness. A community of faith that does not try to mold history is not only undependable but, in the end, impotent.

My second example evokes the oft-heard plaintive question, What can one or two of us possibly do for a better world? At our 1982 General Assembly, Unitarian Universalists saluted Jo and Nick Seidita, a middle-aged California couple, for their extraordinary efforts in the nuclear weapons freeze movement. In December 1980, Nick drafted the nuclear weapons freeze resolution, which was overwhelmingly adopted, along with a plan for implementation by our 1981 General Assembly. Not content to sit back and wait, Jo and Nick began in their own Pacific Southwest UU district to build support. Meanwhile, they inspired their own UU congregation in Sepulveda to contribute $3,000 toward the initiation of the California Freeze Campaign.

With this seed money, through home petition parties and the help of hundreds who volunteered, they sent packets to social studies teachers in every accredited high school in California. Meanwhile, for several months Jo worked full time as a volunteer organizer for the California Nuclear Weapons Freeze Referendum. Despite vigorous opposition by the Reagan administration, the freeze was approved by a substantial majority.

They were only two, but Nick and Jo Seidita, with the support of their congregation, reached out to the Unitarian Universalist Association, and to their entire state, to influence dramatically the growing awareness of and commitment to the need for freezing and reversing the nuclear arms' race. The citation given to them closed with these words: "With pride and pleasure we present the 1982 Holmes-Weatherly Award to Jo and Nick Seidita of Sepulveda, California: committed workers for peace, who have inspired and organized, and shown us the way. May their efforts and ours continue until the ground swell for nuclear control passes from a dream into reality."

Religion Must Be Acted Out

The two examples of acting out our religion, corporately and personally, were known to me intimately and firsthand. I might have chosen and examined scores of others with similar results. A few who think and act clearly and intelligently, and who feel deeply their spiritual responsibility, possess influence vastly out of proportion to their numbers. In whatever concrete ways they may decide to exercise their power, the vital matter to remember is the foundations on which that power rests:

> Religion is concerned with the *all* of life. The world is not cut into two mutually exclusive segments—one containing secular affairs that religion must disregard, the other composed of religious beliefs and rituals.
>
> Religion sees all humankind riding in the same boat, not bobbing about on a lot of separate life rafts bearing the la-

bels "denominations," "nations," "cultures," or "races." We ride out the storms together, or we go down together.

It is not enough for us to profess oneness with others; we must act it out. More than wearing the garment of religious identification, we must welcome its ethical and moral responsibilities.

The substance of religion is in persons who deeply yearn to learn what is good and how it may be obtained; it is not merely the claim of personal sacredness, but the binding of oneself to others through respect and sensitivity toward the sacredness of all. It is not enough to boast of the gift of rational intelligence. The substance of religion is to nurture reason—to work it, to apply it, and to defend it.

My colleague and friend, William F. Schulz, wrote:

If the equation (Plato's) "Being = Power" holds for individuals, then it is even more evident a characteristic of institutions. By its very being-in-the-world the church possesses power. By their property and their wealth; by their prestige and by their people; by their ministries, mailing lists and mimeos; by their visibility and by their vision, our local societies and our Association are *de facto* possessors of power. We cannot avoid it.

So, the issue is never whether or not we possess power, or whether or not we can use it. We do, and we can. What is impossible is avoiding its use. Not to decide in the face of injustice is to decide to let injustice stand. The issue, then, is always how best to decide on the side of our ideals, how best to incarnate in our actions what we stand for.

The Courage to Be

Keep your heart with all diligence, for out of it are the issues of life.

—*Proverbs*

There is no faith without separation.

—Paul Tillich

Christmas is often a perverse reminder of the many reasons we have for feeling unjoyous. Our Unitarian Universalist forebear, Charles Dickens, captured the essence of this experience and of overcoming it in *A Christmas Carol*.

The central characters begin as cogs. Bob Cratchit is not really a person, but a tool, a thing, a machine, hired to turn out as much work as possible. Scrooge is a stick figure, fashioned of cupidity, alienation, and self-hate. Both live in a social situation of moral anarchy. Dickens's answer, appropriate to the crisis, is that love can overcome such radical alienation and weave bonds even between people who lack shared customs and beliefs.

We know that Dickens brought off the miracle of showing Scrooge the power of love, the courage to be new. We face a task more difficult than Scrooge's or Dickens's, not only because our task is real, but because the forces of estrangement and spiritual

165

numbness are stronger now than in the London of Tiny Tim. In a way this can be turned to our advantage, for we have no choice but to recognize and accept the implications of our predicament.

The love that saved Scrooge is now a necessity, not just an option, and it must be love in the tough and universal sense of community and of daring, personal transformation. A fragmented, holocaust-prone world needs people capable of such love to put it together. This putting together is not an abstraction. It needs to be present and real, right now.

I am grateful to *Good News*, the publication of the Unitarian Universalist Christian Fellowship, for the story of a small boy, alone in his bed in the dark. He was afraid, so he called his Dad. Seizing the teachable moment, his Dad said: "My son, you need not fear. God is everywhere. God is with you." And with that he left. Soon the boy was crying again. And again Dad came, administered the same good advice: "Don't be afraid. God is near," and he left. But yet a third time the fear rose, and the boy cried out. This time, the Dad with ever so slight an edge in his voice, asked him: "Son, what did I tell you?" and was told, "Yes, Dad, I know God is everywhere, but sometimes I need someone with skin."

There is power to create in our life circles, intimate and remote, precious bonds of tough and universal love. But it isn't easy. We all know that. We have to incarnate love within our skins.

For many of us, the inexorable limits of life are never more apparent or gripping than in the midst of the Christmas season. We know, for example, that we will never be great as the world measures greatness. We know that we will never be truly saintly. We know that we will never be untainted by life's corrosions, compromises, and hypocrisies. We will never be immune to aging, illness, grievous losses, and bereavements, to crises large and small, to vanished hopes and broken dreams.

The one thing we do need to know, and to encourage one another to know, is what I find at the heart of Dickens's story. It is not God who drives us into anxiety and depression over what is lacking within our skins. We do that to ourselves and to one another. The only status, the only real possibility we need is the one we already have. And we have it as a gift. The gift of life. God is not up there, out there, or everywhere, demanding that we prove ourselves worthy of the gift, only that we express ourselves as conscious receivers of the gift. What a different world we would live in if all of us did that—proving less, expressing more of our simple appreciation, in courage and faithfulness, for that gift of life which is incarnated within our skins. Think how much less anxiety, depression, and weariness there would be! Until then, we are at war with ourselves, making casualties of others.

I have written with fervor in this volume about the blessings of community. I will write more before I finish. But for a few pages, I want to meditate as powerfully as I can upon the individuals who make up communities.

It is as persons, within our self-contained skins, that we experience the ultimate sense of uniqueness and the ultimate anguish of aloneness. The marks of our selfness are unequivocally stamped upon our behavior, whether we are assembled in community or off on a stroll alone. How we walk, sound, write letters, turn our heads is infallibly unique. No one is quite like any other. We are unduplicatable individuals. When we gather in communities, each of us asserts and speaks the lines of an identity that is unique. This takes a great deal of time and energy. To the extent that we permit ourselves to become caricatures of our uniqueness, it is difficult for communities to get much done. We need not become caricatures of ourselves. The best way to avoid it is to do some solid thinking about our uniqueness as aloneness.

Is it really true that each of us is alone? Is not our aloneness largely dissolved in the intimacies of love and fellowship? Do not an ideally married couple overcome separateness? "Love consists in this," wrote Rainer Maria Rilke in *Letters to a Young Poet*, "that two solitudes protect, and touch, and greet one another." Because we are human, we remain alone even in the most affectionate unions. We do not penetrate (indeed, we have no right to try to penetrate) into one another's innermost center of being, no matter how strong our love, because it is our human greatness to have an unassailable inner core which is ours alone.

I went through an uncomfortable period in our denomination when many became engulfed in the encounter movement and obsessed with a need to have everyone "let it all hang out." There is much good to be gained from the insights of this movement. But there is a danger in it, difficult to guard against. It is the danger of trashing something very precious to me in my religious affiliation: recognition and respect for the *impenetrable* center of every person's being. Like anyone else, I have inhibitions, which others can help me overcome. But an ultimate solitude of soul in which to find my deepest convictions is the reality of my being, not an inhibition. This is another way of saying that creation may be a badly botched job, but I love it. I stand alone in creation, encased within my own mortal skin, and, wonder of wonders, I am conscious of this because I am a person. Knowing that I stand separate, I can look out upon the world and love it and cooperate with others who also stand separate, to savor and transform it. This, I say, as Paul Tillich did, is where faith enters and makes its presence profoundly felt. Only as I have the courage to accept my supreme aloneness and vulnerability can I turn to full participation. Only as I am brave enough to know that, even in my own warm home I am but on a visit, only as I can face the fact that everything I build will someday crumble am I free to give that which endures on this earth, the spirit in which I live my life and do my part. This I pass on to my wife, my children and grandchildren, my friends, my parishioners, my colleagues and associates. I live so that the human spirit may live in the only way it can live—within the human skin. Any faith smaller than this will not console me in my transitory defeats, nor comfort me in my times of despair, nor give me the courage to push through.

Shakespeare has Brutus say to Cassius in *Julius Caesar*:

> There is a tide in the affairs of men,
> Which, taken at the flood, leads on to fortune;
> Omitted, all the voyage of their life
> Is bound in shallows and in miseries.

I do not believe that there is any *one* moment that "taken at the flood," leads us to the fulfilling courage to stand and be ourselves. All we are and believe, all we do and work for and love, is constantly under the threat of "shallows" and "miseries." Yet the tides keep rising. We salvage. We compensate. We cultivate the strength that comes with sharing, with caring, with reaching out, with bestowing, where we can, the meanings we discover in the core of our aloneness. This is the truth of Whitehead's famous definition that religion is what we do with our "solitariness." There is reverence in my religion for my solitariness. There is no compulsion in liberal religion to intrude upon my aloneness with public revelations and salvation systems. My solitariness is honored. There is respect for my experience of the human condition and for the way in which I choose to enter into communion with others. There is recognition that the real religious decision for me is what I decide to do, together with others, and that the role of the church is not to bend my will but to give strength and flexibility to my willing. The will is in the self. Out of the self comes the character of the deeds that make for individuality.

In our intermediate fate, there is no substantial variety, because we are all subject to anxiety, accident, and disappointment. In our ultimate fate, there is no variety whatsoever, because we all must die. But it matters greatly how we deal with our anxieties, accidents, and disappointments. It matters greatly what we believe in while we are around. It matters to us, even if it may not matter to the universe, what purposes we set for the days of our years. I am a Unitarian Universalist because I do not require or want revelatory proof of purpose. I have faith in purpose in the midst of the unknown because I know that the purposes I choose in my aloneness are themselves sources of courage, balance, and compensation.

To live is to grow, and to grow means to change enough to be able to play a creative part in change itself. I am acquainted with a play-therapy clinic for children, where the first reaction of one child who was brought for treatment was to raise his arm in protection or attack whenever an adult approached. Flight or fight.

One of the therapists worked and worked with this child until that exquisite moment when an accepting smile finally broke through on the boy's face, and he dropped his arm, his symbol of fear.

The history books will never celebrate this therapist as one of earth's great liberators. Her name will never be joined with Sojourner Truth, Emma Goldman, and Margaret Sanger, but in essence, she is a liberator of the most precious human qualities: courage and trust. In this, she deserves to rank with the greatest, because she shares the emancipating intentions of those who are greatest. And so may we all.

I cannot prove the purposes through which we find the courage to take our stand on the side of life. I do believe in these purposes, and not just naively. I believe in them because I am so sure of the liberating possibilities in men and women. The comfort of my religion rests not on any of the conventional but questionable "proofs" of God's personal concern and care, but on the encouragement I find in my aloneness, and in an appreciation of the aloneness of others, to accept and trust life without such proofs. If the world of nature is impersonal, so be it. If the universe plays no favorites—as Einstein put it, "God does not play dice"—isn't that after all a necessary condition of whatever dependability we can find? My liberal religion offers me the comfort of spiritual solitude in a world where I can rise in hope to meet, or compensate for, most of my problems, where, in fact, I can intelligently anticipate many of the stresses I must solve or bear. In brief, mine is a religion that cares more about me as a person—my potential resources and strengths—than it does about theological explanations or atonements of the dilemmas and failures that beset me. My courage to be is not mediated by priests or revelations. It is cultivated in the recesses of my essential aloneness and challenged by the opportunities of communion with others. I know that my ultimate fate is not in my hands, but my human version of fate is. The element of tragedy I cannot always control, but beyond tragedy I may choose the purposes by which my life will be guided. My human limitations I cannot abolish, but within the limitations are the meanings I am free to create.

I count it as one of the great and good fortunes of my generation that a superb poet, yearning for a metaphor of the twentieth century's spiritual dilemmas, turned to the Book of Job. In writing *J.B.*, Archibald MacLeish ran a literary gauntlet. The Book of Job is probably the most sublime piece of Hebrew literature that has come down to us. It is no small problem to do justice in a modern work to its insight, its imagery, its richness of symbolism, and its depth of feeling. MacLeish has given us a worthy Job of our time, and he tests his fidelity in terms of our calamities and explanations. In a highly imaginative setting, MacLeish successfully avoids sanctimoniousness and religious sentimentality without losing any of the intimacy of the grandeur of J.B.'s terrible trials. I love the way he has Zuss and Nickles play God and Satan by donning a pair of appropriate masks. It is wonderful to have them speaking through their masks with heavenly detachment and then removing their masks to make very human and salty comments about supernatural affairs. The masks produce what is for me one of the most moving perceptions of the entire drama. Nickles, after putting his mask on for the first time, tears it off in a kind of cold sweat. "Those eyes *see*," he says.

They see the *world*. They see it.
From going to and fro in the earth.
From walking up and down, they see it.
I know what Hell is now—to *see*.
Consciousness of consciousness . . .

Has anyone ever experienced a moment of searing, conscious insight without knowing what Nickles meant when he ripped off his mask? To know life is to *see*—to be gripped by the terrible pain and wonder of it.

As a poet, MacLeish was very much of this world. His J.B. is also very much of this world. J.B. is a hearty, prosperous business executive, surrounded by a Hallmark-card family of bright, healthy children, and loved by an intelligent, attractive wife. He thinks well of his fellows and is sincerely grateful to God for his abundance and good fortune. Then God begins to enlighten him about the true nature of life. Afflictions stab with senseless abandon and brutality. One by one his children are destroyed. To cap all this, his business is wiped out, leaving him penniless and suffering from hideous radiation burns. In a final blow, his wife walks out on him for failing to defend himself.

At this point, MacLeish introduces the typical soothsayers of our generation—a Marxist, a psychoanalyst, and a conventional preacher—who explain J.B.'s catastrophes and console him with their characteristic panaceas. His first comforter, the Marxist, tells J.B. that he is being punished by historical necessity:

> God is History. If you offend Him
> Will not History dispense with you?
> History has no time for innocence.

The second comforter, the psychoanalyst, informs J.B. that he is punishing himself unnecessarily in depths of unconscious, mindless guilt.

The third, a ponderous, pastoral type, insists that J.B. is being punished for the unpardonable sin of having been born:

> . . . Guilt is reality!
> The one reality there is!
> All mankind are guilty always!

J.B., in his misery, rejects all three. "What is my fault?" he cries. "What have I done?" The clergyman thunders back:

> What is your fault? Man's heart is evil!
> What have you done? Man's will is evil!
> Your fault, your sin, are heart and will:
> . . . . Your sin is
> Simple. You were born a man!

J.B. crouches lower in his rags and agony, and speaks very softly:

> Yours is the crudest comfort of them all,
> Making the Creator of the Universe

The miscreator of mankind—
A party to the crimes He punishes . . .

At this point MacLeish makes the same abrupt switch we find in the ancient Book of Job. God relents and rewards J.B. for his unwavering loyalty. He restores to J.B. his wife, family, affluence, and health. To say that this resolution cheats is to put it mildly.

What really matters in J.B., as it does in Job, is not that a happy ending is awkwardly patched on, but that there is an epilogue of interpretations and affirmations that go to the heart of the human dilemma. There are, first, the unforgettable words placed in God's mouth by the authors of Job and retained nearly intact by MacLeish:

Where wast thou when I laid the foundations of earth . . .
Hast thou commanded the morning
Can'st thou bind the sweet influence of the Pleiades?

Who are humans to feel that they must have an explanation for everything? Who are humans to believe that their pain and pleasure can only be understood as reward and punishment, as the willful giving or withholding of their God? Is it humans who give the horse strength or make the eagle rise? Reward and punishment are not God's themes; they are human themes. The universe does not reward or punish; it simply is. God does not reward or punish. God is.

And to this J.B. and his wife respond, as we, if we have the wisdom, will also respond. Into any life may come events too terrible to understand, but not because they were willed by a malignant universe. The universe is neither just nor unjust; the universe does not bless or curse. The human answer is not to seek justice in the heavens, but to seek it in the human frame. "You wanted justice, and there was none," J.B.'s wife says. But she offers her love.

The universe gives life—the precious gift of life—and the human response is love: love of God, love of the universe, for making life possible, and love of all those who share the gift. This kind of love is the seat of justice. It is wholly that of humans to give or withhold.

In this violent century, J.B. and J.B.'s wife are abstracts of each and every one of us. As such they are written larger than life, so that their plight overwhelms us not only with pity and terror, but also with reverence for the human race. We are human and we are mortal. We did not create the universe, and we need not despair that we cannot explain all its mysteries and paradoxes. We know that human suffering is pervasive, that it can come to us, and that when it does we must bear it and cope with it. We know also that it comes to others, and that when it does, our task is not to justify or judge but to ease and comfort and uphold. We are born into a world of many evils for human beings. In some of them, we are directly implicated. In some of them, we are not. Our task is not so much to know from whence these evils come, as how they may be resisted, or borne, or overcome.

We speak of justice, but the lesson of Job and J.B. is that the only justice we will find is that which is fashioned by the human spirit. We speak of love, but the lesson of Job and J.B. is that the only love we will know is that which we exchange with one another. The Book of Job was written to challenge the monstrous doctrine that God willfully and personally rewards and punishes. J.B. was written to remind us that if we look to heaven for an explanation of our generation's travails and terrors we will find only emptiness and despair. The universe creates but does not legislate. Justice is a human genius, not a divine one. It may err and be corrected. Misfortune is a human experience, not a cosmic punishment. If all things are to come out right in the end, we do not know it. What we do know is that there is no substitute for blowing on the coals of the human heart.

The answer to what we call the injustices of life is love—our love of life in spite of life. The universe gives life, and humans give life soul, but only if they love in the midst of their thralldom, in spite of suffering, injustice, and death. From Job to J.B. the lesson is this: We are *not* called upon to justify the ways of God; we are always called upon to justify our own ways.

In Job and J.B. I find stirring parables of what my religion means to my courage to be. I do not love life because God will take care of me. My reason tells me that the universe is not organized to look after my personal welfare. The universe has given me life. By placing that life in a body separate from all other bodies, the universe has also granted me an unassailable core of inner being that is mine and mine alone to cultivate and deepen. No priest or revelation can mediate between my solitariness and life as a whole. I love life because, although it leaves me in an ultimate sense alone, it brings me into communion with everyone else's aloneness. In solitariness I sense how intimately I am linked to all those from whom I am separated. My religion is the finding of self and others. It is not only my courage to be myself, in all my stark individuality and aloneness, but also my basic source of the power to live serviceably with others.

Immortality for Skeptics

What happens to this life I prize so highly when, in me, it dies? What befalls this core of inner being that is mine and mine alone when death overtakes my body? Is death the end, or is it a beginning? One of our pamphlets, *Unitarian Universalist Views of Death and Immortality*, presents six personal testimonies, widely different in spirit, tone, and substance. It dramatizes the range of beliefs around which we encourage discussion, open and frank, in our religious community. Such discussions, and my reflections on them, have brought me to the views I share with you here. They are mine. May they be of some help in sorting out your own.

Those who find sustaining hope in the Christian doctrine of personal immortality are struggling in their own way with a universal problem. I do not find this doctrine to be helpful, but I level no charge of self-delusion against those who do. We live in a universe of fantastic possibilities, and with each passing year developments in the physical sciences make the possibilities even more fantastic. I have dealt too long and too intimately with people facing death to feel anything but compassion and sympathy for the various means by which faith and fortitude are mobilized.

I summon to mind sitting at the bedside of a friend who knew that within days cancer would snuff out his life. I asked how he felt about what lay ahead. He told me that he was able to feel quite serene about death. He felt, with Socrates and Elisabeth Kübler-Ross, that death cannot be a harsh or evil thing. He went on: "I would be less than honest, however, if I did not tell you I have qualms about *dying*." Again, the distinction between death and dying I wrote of in an earlier chapter. How valid a distinction it is. Death is unknown, but it is the destiny of all living creatures. Death is either nothingness or another realm of being, and surely neither merits terror. We remain alone in our anticipations of dying. No communication with others can remove this aloneness. Those who love us can touch and protect, but they cannot share or hide the fact that it is our dying and ours alone that awaits. Can we stand this? The world's many theologies of immortality and afterlife bear witness to our doubt that we can stand it without the comfort of a faith certain.

Yet, there are those of us who find small solace in promises of resurrection and eternal life. Most religious liberals are among this group. I myself am unimpressed by the traditional Easter message. It seems to me to be a quite inadequate way of celebrating spring's renewal and rebirth. My ministry is basically to those whose thoughts and experiences lead them to question the Christian faith in resurrection and a personal, eternal, heavenly afterlife, and to seek something more nearly suited to their emotional and rational needs. There is nothing strange or perverse in this point of view. It grows on a person with reflection. It may flicker first as a reaction against the Christian gospel. If Jesus was a divine being, his rising from the dead says nothing about a mere human's ability to conquer death. People are not deities; they are human beings. To celebrate the resurrection of a deity tells us nothing about the prospects for human beings. In good logic, only those who disbelieve in the deity of Jesus should be able to derive any real comfort from the story of his resurrection. It seems to have no proper place in a contemporary, rational view of reality. That early Christians believed in a resurrection is no sound reason, in itself, for believing it today. Everybody believed in supernatural happenings and wonders two thousand years ago. They believed, for example, that mental illness was caused by an invasion of tiny devils into a person's body. In spite of the tremendous amount we still don't understand about mental illness, we at least know that miniature devils are not the explanation. It can be said with much the same reassurance that we also know better about resurrections. Moreover, our study of history makes clear that Jesus did not bring the hope of personal afterlife into the world, because not only the hope but the belief in it was held by peoples long before his time.

Elisabeth Kübler-Ross now numbers herself among those who tell us that, quite aside from Jesus's role, there is a growing body of clinical evidence of personal immortality. There are reputable researchers who work full-time on the remembered experiences of patients who returned to life after being "medically" dead. These accounts have a ring of authenticity about them and reassuring descriptions of personally felt peace, serenity, and beauty. But after examining this literature, an honest mind can conclude that it is still speculation, not proof.

There have long been impressive forms of poetically expressed beliefs in personal survival after death. They come from persons, such as Evelyn Underhill and William Wordsworth, who base their faith on what they call intimations and intuitions of inner experience. Emerson had similar feelings and wrote:

> What is excellent,
> As God lives, is permanent;
> Hearts are dust, heart's loves remain;
> Heart's love will meet thee again.

Yet, even under the spell of beautiful thoughts so beautifully expressed, there are some of us who are not persuaded by our sense of human worth to require a personal continuance after death. In other words, traditional concepts of immortality do not become more valid simply because they are associated with a morally satisfying view of human life. Feeling, of itself, no matter how elevated, does not signify personal survival. Compassionate human behavior is not inspiring because it whispers to us of some concrete plan of immortality; it is inspiring in itself and on its own merits. The teachings of Jesus are not guides to ethical growth because they are linked to beliefs about his resurrection. They are guides because their worth is implicit in human conduct.

Why I exist, nobody on earth is capable of telling me, but since I do exist, let me strive to give my existence a brightness and glory by setting for myself the loftiest goals I can reasonably hope to achieve. This is my religious view. Is there a kind of immortality that fits and augments such a view? To me there is, and I am joined in it by many of my fellow Unitarian Universalists. Interestingly enough, there is nothing new about this view. Since long before the time of Jesus it has been cultivated by some of the Chinese religions. It has been known and cherished by Buddhists for nearly twenty-five hundred years. It is belief in the immortality of character, of conduct and thought, of influence. In no way does this take from me the loneliness of dying. I know that dying is something I must face alone and with honest apprehension. But I have something to live and die for: not a personal survival, which would (and may) greatly surprise me, but a present and lasting immortality of influence in which I can and do believe.

Whatever such an observation may be worth, this is truly a democratic idea of immortality. It is an affirmation that everyone is immortal since whatever we do lives on somehow, somewhere, somewhen. The evil we do is as immortal as the good. There is an immortality of the ignoble as well as the noble, of the brutish as well as the sublime, of selfishness as well as generosity, of stupidity as well as wisdom. Immortality is complete. It encompasses the whole of what one is.

When we reason together about the truths and mysteries of life, there is one all-powerful reality: The humanity of which we are individual expressions is a product of the sense and nonsense of our forebears. We are the living immortality of those who came before us. In like manner, those who come after us will be the harvest of the wisdom and folly we ourselves are sowing. To let this reality permeate and drench our consciousness is to introduce ourselves to a grand conception of immortality which makes yearnings for some form of personal afterlife seem less consequential. So long as there is an ongoing stream of humanity I have life. This is my certain immortality. I am a renewed and renewing link in the chain of humanity. My memory and particularity are personal, transitory, finite; my substance is boundless and infinite. The immortality in which I believe affirms first and foremost my unity with humankind. My unity with humankind gives meaning to my desire to practice reverence for life. It is pride in being and pride in belonging to all being. I do not welcome the fact that dying waits for me. Yet, I know that I must die, and I will attempt to do so with all the fortitude and dignity circumstances and forethought permit.

Death, on the other hand, presents me with no special problem. It cannot be an evil condition. Of immortality, my mind and heart cherish the kind I have described. My religious community affirms rather than denies the freedom with which I have discussed these matters. As a Unitarian Universalist I grant that there may be a personal existence after death. Many of my coreligionists believe there is. No one can really tell. But there is one assured immortality, the realism of which we can know in advance. It connects us with every human being who shares this earth with us. It joins us in unbroken line with all who have mortally passed from this earth before us. It unites us with all who are yet to be born. By the glow of this idea of immortality, I have long aided and abetted Helen Caldicott's crusade against the nuclear arms race, and I resonate with her words:

> It is time for people to rise to their full moral and spiritual height, to take the world on their shoulders like Atlas . . . and to say *I* will save the earth. . . . No other generation has inherited this enormous responsibility and the privilege of saving all past and all future generations. Think of the variety of delicate butterflies; of the gorgeous birds, of the fish in the sea; of the flowers; of the proud lions and tigers and of

the wondrous prehistoric elephants and hippopotamuses; think of what we are about to destroy (*Missile Envy*).

For those of us who can no longer live under the spell of traditional beliefs in resurrections and personal afterlives, the larger message of immortality need not be lost. Fundamentally, it is a message of renewed, redeemed, ongoing life and of the wonder that our thoughts and deeds are our real immortality.

If Jesus Is the Answer

They pop into view all over the continent—signboards, billboards, and bumper stickers bearing the message "Christ Is the Answer." If Christ is the answer, what are the questions? An answer, unless it is preceded by a meaningful question, is not much of an answer. One of Steve Allen's old routines, "The Question Man," satirized the vacuity of quiz programs and games. Appearing as a seedy, rumpled professorial type, Allen provided the questions for people's answers. Behind the satire is a basic truth. It is frequently easier to supply answers than it is to ask the right questions. Unitarian Universalism is an "asking" religion, and unashamedly so. There are no qualms about asking what should be a very obvious question: How do we know who Jesus is or was?

The answer must be discovered in the writings about him, and these are the Gospels. Nothing is known of Jesus except what is found in them. All other literature of his time and place is lacking in a single, meaningful reference. The letters of Paul have much to say *about* Jesus, but Paul acknowledges that he never knew Jesus in the flesh. What Paul wrote was interpretation. If this is true of Paul, it is even more true of at least one of the Gospels, John. If Paul was far removed from the personality of Jesus, then John, according to most scholars, was even further removed. So, what we have left to answer our question must be found in Matthew, Mark, and Luke. We know nothing about these books from any independent source, and we know little if anything about their authors. Scholars generally agree that the names Matthew, Mark, and

Luke have meager historical credibility. Whatever validity these Gospels possess must be confirmed within the text of the books themselves. When we turn to an examination of the Gospel material, we find that in large part the three are identical, so that the whole material about Jesus is about one-third of what it seems to be. Most scholars believe that Matthew and Luke copied extensively from Mark and that what is distinctive in their accounts came from written recollections that have never been recovered. This suggests that Matthew and Luke had no first-hand knowledge of Jesus. But what about Mark? Did he know Jesus in the flesh? If he did, the acquaintanceship must have been distant. There is not a single reference in Mark to the appearance or mannerisms of Jesus, something that seems unlikely if the author had had contact with such an apparently vivid personality. We are forced to conclude that the author of Mark's Gospel could have known people who *did* know Jesus, and he may even have been a younger contemporary. Matthew and Luke wrote a generation later, and John nearly a century later.

Having taken this quick tour through the scholarly realms of New Testament study, we find some questions to be inescapable. How can a person be the answer about whom there is no first-hand knowledge, and very sparse second- or third-hand information? Historical knowledge may not be the only means of judging, but what other justifications are there for the claim that Jesus is the answer?

Intelligent, sensitive, dedicated people, who are fully aware of the implications of biblical scholarship, still say that Jesus is the answer, as they did when the World Council of Churches met in Vancouver in the summer of 1983. We, who are puzzled by this, owe it to ourselves to try to understand their position. One fruitful approach is to acquaint ourselves with how heavily Christian theologians lean on a Danish genius of the nineteenth century, Søren Kierkegaard, who probed the mysteries of faith through the existentialist technique of looking deeply within himself. By doing this, Kierkegaard was convinced that his inner self was a chaos of untruth, sinfulness, and alienation from God. If humans are created in the image of God, how can this be? Kierkegaard insisted that God dwells not within the human frame. Saving grace must come from outside. The deeper we probe into ourselves, the further we are from ultimate truth.

By looking to our own resources, we have widened the gulf between ourselves and God. Sin has conquered our precious free will. The more we struggle to pull ourselves up by our bootstraps to touch the reality of God, the more we sink into a slough of despond. Even a knowledge of God's love overwhelms us and makes us more hopelessly conscious of sin. The only answer is for God to take the initiative. God can do this in two ways. One is to lift humans to the level of God; the other is for God to accept the debasement of becoming human. Kierkegaard argued that the first course is unthinkable. He did not adequately explain why it is unthinkable, but he dismissed the possibility. The second choice is the only defensible one. God, said Kierkegaard, came over to humans by becoming human in the form of Jesus Christ.

This startling act is not without its drawbacks, according to Kierkegaard. The human mind is affronted, and the affront cuts in two directions. Jesus's claim to be the Christ/God is odiously offensive to human reason. Any such claim is insulting. At the same time, it is an attack on human reason to expect that God would dream of becoming human. The mind rebels at the absurdity of God becoming a carpenter whose fate is to die on a cross as a common criminal in the insignificant land of Palestine.

With genuine savor, Kierkegaard shaped the paradox and declared that only the love of God makes it possible for the mind to accept such an irrational truth. But in order to be a Christian, Kierkegaard concluded, you must crush reason and take a leap of faith. Thus, becoming a Christian is an agonizing experience that bears no resemblance to what Kierkegaard called the "perpetual Sunday twaddle about Christianity's . . . sweet consolation." Kierkegaard's Christianity consists of no reasonable summons to tread conventional paths of public piety. It is an uncompromising repudiation of reason in favor of a shattering, transporting faith. This is what makes Jesus the answer, not whether scholarly examination of the Bible delineates and confirms his mission. It is all right for a Christian to be intellectually interested in rational studies of religion, but salvation is another matter. Without the leap of faith, there is no salvation. Jesus is the answer not in reason but in faith.

Kierkegaard sharpens the issue magnificently and makes the next question inescapable. Am I prepared to leave reason behind to go soaring into what he calls faith? The answer, obviously, is a resounding no. I have no argument with the notion that Kierkegaard was an authentic font of Christian theology, but he has failed to persuade me to abandon my mind. I do have a mind. It may not be an overly impressive one, but such as it is, it is mine. However I may have come to possess it—whether from God, or from genes and chromosomes, or from culture and education, or from a combination of all these and more—I am determined to make the best of it in my religious life. If rational intelligence is part of my given endowment, it is logically given to be exercised rather than exorcised. If Jesus is the answer only if I cast out my reasoning abilities, he cannot be the answer for me.

Fair enough, my orthodox friends may say. You cannot accept by a leap of faith that Jesus is the answer. What about his unsurpassed moral teachings? Can't your reason accept these as an authentic revelation of God's saving power?

Historically, Unitarian Universalists have professed reverence for the teachings of Jesus. In fact, an idealized interpretation of Jesus as teacher and prophet has characterized our development and still does. Some among us consider themselves to be true Christians, not in a Kierkegaardian sense, but in terms of the reverence in which they hold and desire to emulate the teachings of Jesus. In the last decade and a half, our ranks, Christian and non-Christian alike, have been deeply challenged by Christian liberation theology. Arising first in Latin America, then in the larger Third World, then among blacks, women, youth, and gays, liberation theology has mightily empowered Christian commitment to the poor, the dispossessed, the scorned, and the abused. To liberation theology, Christianity in its most fundamental impulse is a religion of the underdog, and Jesus is the supreme symbol of that impulse. In Jesus is found the ultimate person "for others"—the saving exemplar of total commitment, in love and sacrifice, to the struggles of one's fellow beings. Jesus is "the place to be." And the place of this Christ is in the midst of the struggle for justice, political empowerment, and peace. It is in the world, in the midst of human sin, suffering, and degradation, with the needy and oppressed.

If our Unitarian Universalist religion means anything, it means the right to choose this kind of identification with Jesus. Many of us have been moved by it. Still there are difficulties; not with the prophetic commitments of Christian liberation theology, but with the role assigned to the teachings of Jesus. If the teachings of Jesus are the answer, which teachings and which Jesus is meant? "Render unto Caesar that which is Caesar's, and unto God that which is God's" (Matthew 22). According to the Gospels, Jesus taught it, but where in it is encouragement to stand against the Caesars of this world?

An attentive reading of the Gospels can be an unnerving experience. When Jesus called for turning the other cheek, he seemed not to allow for compelling exceptions. There are many situations in which turning the other cheek is not only moral but highly practical conduct. On other occassions it might be a way of risking not only one's own safety but that of others as well. If I spotted a man about to detonate an explosive in a crowded Boston subway station, I would be inclined to try to stop him forcibly. Turning the other cheek has something less than universal application in struggles to overturn painful injustices.

It can be argued that Jesus believed in the ultimate conquest of good over evil and based his teaching on such a belief. I happen to believe that there is nothing inevitable about this. In fact, most of the good that counts is doggedly and forcefully implemented. What I am saying is simply that I am against turning the other cheek when it is stupid and unreasonable to do so. On the other hand, I recognize how plausible and effective turning the other cheek can be in a large percentage of the stresses that afflict ordinary human relations. I attempt, therefore, to practice it, subject to the guidance of reason and situation, and I honor Jesus for the advocacy of it. Then I remember that in another portion of the Gospels Jesus used excessively violent language against the Pharisees and Sadducees. No cheek turning there. Which was the real Jesus? Was he both or neither? "Do not think that I have come to bring peace, but a sword. For I have come to set a man against his father, and a daughter against her mother, and a daughter-in-law against her mother-in-law; and a man's foes will be those of his own household" (Matthew 10:34–36). Can this be the same Jesus who in the same Gospel is reported to have said: "Love your enemies. . . ."?

The logical inference is that the true followers of Jesus will stir up hostilities even within their own families but will proceed to love the enemies they have made. In truth, there is no logic in a juxtaposition of these two teachings except the logic of anyone's human inconsistencies. But if these are two sides of Jesus's personality, which am I to accept as the answer?

Actually, what religious liberals generally have in mind when they speak of their reverence for the moral leadership of Jesus are his most apt and penetrating parables, plus that remarkable collection of sayings in Chapters 5, 6, and 7 of the Gospel of Matthew, known misleadingly as the Sermon on the Mount. I can warmly endorse the notion that these are moving and inspiring ethical teachings. I cannot, however, close my mind to other teachings attributed to Jesus, which strike me as being anything but ennobling. Taking the Gospel narratives as they stand, Jesus believed in hell. As you know, I do not myself feel that anyone who is deeply humane can believe in everlasting punishment. But Jesus as depicted in the Gospels did believe in it, and one finds his fury vented on those who would not heed his preaching—a mode of expression, some would say, that is not uncommon among preachers, but that does raise questions. We find the Gospels placing on Jesus's lips: "You serpents, you generation of vipers, how can you escape the damnation of hell?" To my mind, this is not the most admirable tone he might have taken.

The point I am trying to make, and it seems to me to be a very important one, is that the Jesus portrayed in the Gospels is an elusive figure, as Albert Schweitzer so amply demonstrated. What we really seem to mean when we say that the "spirit of Jesus" is the answer to our problems is that we would like to try to the best of our ability to live by the moral precepts we choose to identify with Jesus. Christian liberation theologians do it their way, and they have my empathy. The Jerry Falwells of this world do it their way, and they do not have my empathy. Many of my coreligionists identify with the moral goals Jesus represents to them, namely compassion, unselfishness, self-sacrifice, love, faithfulness, and goodwill. No one should be upset if I suggest that the admirable goals represented by this chosen idealization of Jesus can be duplicated in all of the world's great religions.

Jesus is, and will remain, an enduring idealization of much that religious liberals hold dear in the religious life. By the same token, religious liberals should be as anxious to avoid fuzzy thinking about Jesus as about other religious symbols. The book is not closed on questions and answers about Jesus. The Dead Sea Scrolls brought fresh excitement to the subject. Other finds of similarly provocative material may well turn up.

To me, the important thing about Jesus is not that he was *just* human, but that the human race is capable of producing him. And not him alone, but others like him. And not only in ancient times, but now.

Let Us Pray

Prayer is both a problem and a challenge to religious liberals. It must have been a problem to my parents, but not much of a challenge. The only prayer they taught me as a small child was the familiar "Now I lay me down to sleep. . . ." I am satisfied that it did me no harm, but it took me many years to conquer negative feelings toward prayer and to find a constructive place for it in my religious life. I still experience waves of revulsion at the content of certain types of public prayer, but I can hear Robert Louis Stevenson with joy and inspiration:

> The day returns and brings us the petty round of irritating concerns and duties. Help us . . . to perform them with laughter and kind faces; let cheerfulness abound with industry. Give us to go blithely on our business all this day, bring us to our resting beds weary and content and undishonored, and grant us in the end the gift of sleep.

This, I would say, is an eminently worthy prayer that anyone could repeat without feeling craven. Like John Tyndall, I think "solemnly of the feeling which prompts prayer. It is a power which I should like to see guided, not extinguished—devoted to practicable objects instead of wasted upon air." Prayer should trouble the conscientious religious liberal. In many of its customary forms, it is primitive, naïve, and frequently selfish. Who can attribute nobility to attempts to cajole and wheedle God into giving us what we personally want, or into bending the order of nature or history for our personal benefit? Mark Twain's Huckleberry Finn was a classic practitioner of the kind of prayer that backlashes. His Aunt Polly gave him a fishing pole. She also told him that if he prayed hard enough, God would hear and respond. Huck took this literally. Several nights in a row he closeted himself in his room and prayed for some fishhooks. He did not receive them. Obviously, there was something wrong with the whole idea of prayer, so Huck gave it up.

This is a familiar problem. It illustrates the importance of the assumptions we make about prayer. If prayer is viewed as a method of getting what we want, as a kind of cosmic lever for prying personally desired answers out of the Almighty, then, like Huck, we are doomed to futility and frustration. Like him, we will renounce prayer as a snare and a delusion, and we would be quite right about this particular kind of praying.

But suppose we start from an entirely different assumption.

Suppose we think of prayer not as a means of commandeering God's attention for our personal wants, but as an approach to the deepest truths about ourselves. Suppose we think of it as a way of shedding new light on our relations with others or with God. Suppose we think of it as an essential religious striving to touch truth and tap resources within and beyond ourselves. What then? Do not great possibilities open before us? I talked recently with a parishioner who was suffering from a series of devastating blows. "The temptation is overwhelming," she told me, "to believe that God has simply abandoned me. Then I remind myself that God doesn't move in and out of our lives, and that the real challenge for me is not to abandon God." There is a heap of wisdom in her words. I will never forget them.

There are many means for getting what we think we want in this world. Money is one. Prestige, power, and privilege are others. There are various kinds of "pull" we can exert. For adults as well as for children, sometimes a tantrum will produce favorable results. Political leverage can often accomplish wonders. Prayer is not like these. Rather, it is an effort to reach deep and to reach out and to *become* what we would like to be, and need to be, and ought to be. Proper prayer is not a petition to escape realities. It is an effort to face up to realities, to understand them, to deal with them. It is an expression of the desire to grow in spiritual stature, in courage, in strength, and in faith. The purpose of prayer is to transform those doing the praying, to lift them out of fear and selfishness into serenity, patience, determination, belonging. If we begin to approach prayer in this manner, it assumes an entirely new significance.

There are many recognitions of this kind of prayer. In an ancient and beautiful book, the *Theologica Germanica*, we read that our purpose in prayer is to "be to the eternal goodness what our own hands are to us." Each person has hidden energies that deserve to be released. Within all of us dwell imprisoned splendors of hope, aspiration, and spiritual transformation. In fact, this particular path of prayer has been worn by the passage, through the ages, of all sorts of men and women who have sought and found an open way to sustain religious truth. Jesus traveled it, and so did Buddha, Lao-tze, Phillis Wheatley, and Gandhi. This is a journey that may be taken by any. Each of the world's religions and races has contributed to our knowledge of the terrain. This inward excursion to the growth and transformation of the human spirit is one of the truest marks of the universality of religion. In spite of all the external differences of the faiths by which humans live, the inward pilgrimage is everywhere much the same. Aldous Huxley called it the perennial philosophy. Buddha named it the noble eightfold path. Others have called it simply "the way." On this journey no one need be separated from others by differences of doctrine. All are friends and companions.

We are first made aware of our need for a deepening of the inward life in various ways. Awareness may arise from a haunting sense of dissatisfaction with ourselves as we are. Or, we may become bored and weary with too much surface activity, which leaves little or no time for thought, reflection, or meditation. We may feel that there must be more comprehensive meanings to life than those we have so far discovered. Our lives may receive a severe shock or a whole series of them, shaking us to the foundations, so we pause and take stock. We ask questions about what we are doing and why we are doing it. We make an effort to find out what our lives should mean, what they do mean, and what they could mean.

Here, in this process of self-examination, the sifting and judging of our desires go on. Here we can slowly learn what is one of the first and deepest lessons of religious growth: that the requirements of love, justice, peacemaking, and truth may well run contrary to some of our personal desires and inclinations. The profoundest fulfillment of our lives is *not* to be found in getting what we think we want, but in giving what is needed. Here we are made humble and eventually wiser. Until we have experienced this process, our religion has not really begun to ripen. It does not much matter how it comes about—in church or out, verbally or silently, invoking God by name or not. What matters is that it *does* happen, and that when it happens we know we are involved in the first, tentative steps of a genuine prayer experience.

Quite rightly, psychologists tell us that these initial, hesitant breakthroughs are fraught with dangers. Self-searching, without positive steps, can lead to self-abasement, discouragement, and despair. We must push beyond our all-too-evident weaknesses and failings. We must find and recognize the strengths we have, and our hopes. This is the seeking aspect of prayer, only it must be a seeking that is disciplined and cleansed of narcissism. As Phillips Brooks expressed it in a sermon: "Do not pray for easy lives. Pray to be stronger. . . . Do not pray for tasks equal to your powers. Pray for powers equal to your tasks." Once entered upon this inward journey, we have an obligation to seek the strength and courage equal to great tasks. This is the positive part of prayer, its outreach. Much honesty of soul is required. There is plenty of space for centering but none for sentimentality in this kind of praying.

Finally, there is the aspect of patience. Lives conditioned to constant activity and diversion do not readily appreciate the value and necessity of simply waiting in silence, in expectation, in appreciation of things to come. One of the most colorful and promising dimensions of the human spirit is its ability to experience sudden flashes of insight and clarity. All at once a sense of direction emerges out of chaos. Formidable obstacles melt away. A decision is suddenly plain. Norbert Wiener used to tell his students that solutions to seemingly insoluble mathematical problems frequently came to him in the dead of night when his mind was presumably at rest.

Sometimes we seem to have nothing to offer but our perplexity, our indecision, our confusion. Then out of the silence, the waiting, the expectation, and the appreciation of things to come, a light breaks through. Is a prayer answered? Yes, but not in a supernatural or miraculous sense. It is simply true that some of our most important moral decisions and spiritual discoveries come upon us with surprise and wonder when we are receptive and ready to use them.

These, then, are aspects of prayer that recommend themselves to a person like myself, who does not hesitate to register his distaste for prayers seeking a winning lottery ticket, victory, safety, fishhooks, or the discomfiting of enemies.

Prayer based on self-examination, on an honest ordering of our minds, and on the ability to wait in expectation and appreciation of untapped and unrevealed spiritual resources, is, to me, prayer at its best. In the words of Lon Ray Call: "Prayer doesn't change things, but it changes people and people change things. Let us pray."

Marcus Borg - Jesus

Index